G000144798

AEROADDICT

The story of one man's lifelong love affair with Aeroplanes
by Doug Gregory D.F.C.

To Brenda the brains behind
the ACC and good enough to
put up with we odd chaps
for Doug

Published by
Little Knoll Press
First imprint – November 2013

ISBN No. 978-0-9927220-0-5

Copies of this book can be obtained
by emailing Jenny@LittleKnollPress.co.uk
online from www.LittleKnollBookshop.co.uk
and from UK bookshops
(Request and order using the title and ISBN No.)

Printed in Great Britain by
CMP Ltd.
Poole, Dorset

FOREWORD
by Julian Lewis
MP for New Forest East

Doug Gregory is one of the two airmen I know who hold the Distinguished Flying Cross. They have three features in common: they put themselves in peril when young; they are diffident about their gallantry; and they behave in maturity as if living on borrowed time.

AEROADDICT will reveal to generations of former Noadswood School pupils, here in the New Forest, a totally different dimension of their much-respected Art Master – namely, his 'lifelong love-affair with aeroplanes' in war and in peace. Doug's flying career has two distinct halves: as a night-fighter pilot over enemy territory and, decades later, as a display pilot in a replica Great War S.E.5a biplane fighter. This, with the unstinting support of his wife Liz, he built in his own back garden and flew at air shows until the age of 90.

Interwoven with the story of his four-year construction of the S.E.5a are Doug's memories as a boy obsessed by aviation, as a volunteer for the RAF aged 18 in 1941, and as a pilot who flew some 90 aircraft in England, Scotland, Africa, India and, most hazardously, over Nazi-occupied Europe.

There is plenty here to fascinate would-be aero-engineers, and plenty more for those intrigued by true stories of adventure. Doug writes humorously about amateur airframe construction, passionately about his loathing of the Nazis, and grippingly about air warfare: *'Each trip to enemy country presented new experiences ... the pangs of dismay when watching a Lancaster flaming down in its death dive ... a great bomber, coned by hundreds of searchlights, unable to extricate itself from the deadly web of beams.'*

At the end of the war he regarded himself as *'an overgrown office boy with still no qualifications, except the ability to kill. I had little to offer.'* Nothing could be further from the truth. Doug Gregory's service to our country and community, as warrior, educator and aerial entertainer, puts us all in his debt. This modest memoir cloaks a dauntless and sensitive spirit – and one which will see him through a few more flights in the months and years to come.

JL

INTRODUCTION
by Doug Gregory D.F.C.

If you are expecting to find within these pages the greatest war book so far written, or if you hope to glean how the war was shortened, or lengthened, by my contribution to it, or if you want the stirring 'Boy's Own stories' kind of yarns, STOP NOW.

This is an account of me, building a fun aeroplane for my enjoyment in my dotage, and while building it, dragging up and jotting down a few reminiscences with which I have bored friends over the years.

Building an aeroplane is fun in itself, but it is only a means to an end. Flying it is the greatest pleasure.

I will go no further before saying a big thank-you to the people who helped me in this venture. It could never be hailed as a one-man show. Without friends who supplied wood and metal, advised, found bits and pieces, welded to the approved standard, turned lumps of metal, ground other lumps, bashed tin, pushed, pulled, lifted and generally gave time and assistance, this project would, literally, never have got off the ground. A special thanks to my wife, Liz, who was my inspiration, task master and helpmate.

DG

CONTENTS

CHAPTER ONE
Building my own aeroplane, the birth of a dream

The clouds invite my presence to their world
And I obey with eagerness and glee,
And venture far, to where their bounds unfurled
So welcome those who struggle to be free.

Up through the valleys of their glistening form
The craft mounts, ready to comply
And turning, shreds the waifish storm
To chase the snowy maidens of the sky.

And then caress the domes and peaks that stand
Above the dewy softness drifting there
So plunge and wallow, grasping out of hand
To feast and languish in the yielding air.

Ah, then begins the final downward glide
The sleepy sliding flight will soon descend
To leave me drained and amply satisfied
And bring me back to earth's mundane end.

So there I was, retired and just had time to build and fly my own aeroplane. We hear a lot, especially from our children, about old fools having a second childhood. I think I must be in mine. Certainly I recall, from my first childhood, at the age of eleven, constructing a quite sizeable model of a First World War fighter. Carving the propeller, making the guns, marking the ribs in the wings, fitting the bracing wires, painting the whole thing to look authentically beautiful and deadly, then putting my eye close up to the cockpit, squinting through the wings and wires and, there I was the other ace, apart from McCudden, Mannock and Ball.

What a beautiful fighter this S.E.5a was. Not so well known as the Sopwith Camel and Pup, not so big as the Bristol Fighter, not so small as the Spad, but a brilliant product of a Mr Folland and his Royal Aircraft Factory team. For a year or two my model sat on the top of my wardrobe where I could see it from my bed. There it was at first light, ready for the dawn patrol, or last thing at night, preparing for 'Home Defence' against the Gothas.

Its shape, firmly impressed on my memory for always, sprang to life a few years ago, when I saw a replica of the S.E.5a fly into Newbury racecourse on a very wet Sunday, landing just behind my Tiger Moth as I taxied soggily to the marshalling point. There was my dream machine, just as I remembered it. Flat-fronted radiator, pugnacious stance, Lewis gun on the top of the top wing, roundels resplendent. What a thrill! I'd love to own such a beautiful aeroplane.

I retired from work at the age of sixty. Life began. I suppose the expression 'life began' is a little too strong; after all, I often felt I'd been living on borrowed time since the 1940's when so many of my contemporaries stopped living. So maybe I should say 'another life began'. Retirement gave me the chance to start doing the things which I had never had time to do whilst being committed to earning a living.

First and foremost, a certain amount of time had to be devoted to bringing the family home to a reasonable state of repair, and to do all those little things I had managed to put off for years. It was mainly decoration inside and outside, and trying to stop the garage from failing down. Really, my idea of the perfect life-style is to have somewhere to eat, somewhere to sleep and then lots and lots of sheds and workshops. To build my aeroplane, a large shed was required, and by a stroke of luck such a shed was for sale in Southampton. This was delivered by two giants, who dragged the large sections from the pavement through to the back garden. It looked enormous, blanking off half the shrubbery and covering a vast amount of lawn.

August bank holiday was spent erecting the thing. I found that by giving a couple of intelligent school-leavers a hammer each and a bag of nails, the battle was half over. Papering the inside with newspaper and whitewashing everywhere gave me the basis for an excellent hangar in which to start building.

Plans for the Replica S.E.5a were ordered from the Popular Flying Association. I suppose by then I could consider I was ready for the off.

I must say that constructing a home-built aircraft would be nearly impossible without the support, organisation and guidance of the Popular Flying Association (now renamed the Light Aircraft Association, or LAA). This body was set up many years ago for the purpose of encouraging home builders to produce a light aircraft which would give their owners pleasure as well as keeping them within strict safety limits. Inspection at many stages of the building of an aircraft by approved aircraft inspectors, keeps all projects at a high level of competence.

So, with plans, books of rules, much heart-searching and some determination, my project began.

Here, I feel, is a good time to introduce my near neighbour, Des. He, another pilot about ten years my junior and a chartered engineer by profession, had the same attitude to light aircraft as myself. Not unnaturally, he decided to build his own Replica S.E.5a at the same time as myself. This double project worked extremely well. Problems shared were problems solved in half the time, materials ordered in duplicate saved a bit in transport expense, but probably the greatest asset was the doubling of enthusiasm to press on with the job. We never at any time reached the point of giving up, which I'm afraid so many home builders reach.

All books on the subject of light aircraft building stress the necessity of 'the table'. How right that is. The table, twelve feet long and two and a half feet wide, made and braced with two inch by two inch angle iron, the top, dead flat and smooth and whitewashed. Onto that is drawn each section of the fuselage to be made, just like the making of the balsa wood models of my youth. All measurements checked and re-checked and, thank God, the measurements were in Imperial, The plans were Canadian, hence the Imperial. I have not yet got round to using those funny metric signs.

During the time waiting for table welding and the delivery of lengths of chipboard for the top, other pieces of machinery were assembled. All my old hand tools were displayed in racks; chisels, saws, clamps, screwdrivers, oilstones, hammers and hacksaws, planes and pliers, all manner of relics from the past, collected from being spread around the various boxes in the various sheds and now brought together in readiness. Two woodwork benches along one side of the hangar supported vices, a drill press, a band saw and a most useful disc sander with extractor fan. I was ready to start.

The Table

I love wood, especially beautiful wood. In the early days of my marriage, when 'contemporary furniture' was all the rage, beautiful woods were the main ingredient of the modern movement, which probably started in Sweden where the manufacturers completely disregarded the traditional materials and used teak, unstained mahogany, beautifully figured plywoods and many others which were rarely considered furniture-usable. I had no hope of buying any of the pieces I had seen in the furniture shops like Maples or Heals, so decided, with great trepidation, to make my own. We are still using some of it, although my solid mahogany coffin-shaped dining table fell to pieces after about twenty years' wear.

The wood I was to use now was very different, but just as beautiful. The cutting list for the fuselage was prepared, taking many hours of searching, measuring, calculating from the plans, and then doubling the whole lot and adding a bit for luck. To collect the long lengths of spruce we, Des and I, borrowed a glider trailer and headed to the wilds of the West Riding, flogging the car along to complete the journey there and back in the short, October daylight.

The wood was beautiful, straight grained, no run out, beautifully prepared by a man who obviously had a great deal more interest in his work than just passing commodities over the counter. So to the first cut. That took a sit down for half an hour with a cup of strong tea before I could bring myself to make the first move. Sod's law, and my usual over-eagerness, guarantees that if mistakes are to be made, I'll make them. Courage restored. In no time the three quarter inch by three quarter inch longerons of the fuselage were laid out onto the table drawing, cross pieces cut and fitted, aerolite glue, made the day before, applied, corner blocks dropped into place. I had started the bird cage of a fuselage. Clamped up, held down, grease proof paper under the gluey bits to stop them sticking to the table; I felt, then, I was committed.

Friends calling were always welcome, even when they stopped me working. After all, their visits were never that long and it nearly always meant a cup of tea. I could hear them approaching, chattering away to Liz, my wife. "What d'you say he's doing, building an aeroplane? Oh, my husband used to build little aeroplanes when we were first married." "Not little aeroplanes, a real one for him to fly in." "Oh." That 'Oh' was long and drawn out and really meant, "I can't think why anybody in their right mind would want to; and how long will it be before he's put away?" Their next remark was always the same. "Is he building it from a kit?" I suppose they expected to look into the shed and see me sticking pieces of black plastic together with Airfix glue.

When they did actually enter, there were more 'Oh's, as I tried to explain that this case of sticks was really upside down, at the moment, and if you could imagine it up the other way, I would eventually be sitting 'there', the petrol tank fits into 'there', and of course there will be an engine on the front, sticking out to 'there'. Exit friend in confusion and probably thinking, 'Poor Liz, that's what all those years of school-mastering have done for him.'

The original S.E.5a of 1917 was built with a wire-braced fuselage, where the whole structure was criss-crossed with wires, which could be adjusted for tension, pulling the body into a very strong shape while remaining comparatively light-weight.

We, thank goodness, were required to box the whole thing in with thin plywood. Scarfing the 1/8th inch ply joints began as a problem, so a scarfing machine was constructed, using a metal cylinder turned down to a low angled cone, covered with glass paper, driven by an electric motor. When the cone was mounted a fraction above the bench top, the plywood was then waltzed through, the surface being skimmed off at an angle to leave about an inch and a half scarf. It worked surprisingly well, though at first the dust from the skimming process was choking everything, especially the operator. This hazard was remedied by attaching the tube of a vacuum cleaner near the cone.

Doug working on the 'tea chest'

The boxing in of the fuselage gave a look of solidity and by the time the front and rear main bulkheads were fitted and the turtle deck in place, even most visitors could distinguish the makings of an aeroplane showing through. I knew from the start that although this was called a wooden aeroplane, quite a lot of metal had to be incorporated in the many, many brackets which held the dozens of essential pieces which were to be hung on. The controls, elevators, rudder, ailerons, brakes, all required brackets, as did the wings, the tail plane and undercarriage. All smaller items like struts, gun sights, petrol tanks, were attached with brackets. I came to loathe brackets. Brackets must be made from the proper specified materials, not any old bit of steel or aluminium. I was learning. In fact, I was required to learn so much that was new to me. After all, what was the British equivalent for 4130 American steel, if there was one, was it S514 or S515 or anything like? What when hardened, or not, and could any of it be machined when hard? What was aluminium 2024-T3 and where can you get it? Who can supply small quantities of the correct specification of tubes? Who sells Fafnir bearings? My head whirled. It was only the fact that Des was a good engineer that these things were explained and eventually sorted out so that by the time those wretched brackets were appearing to do all they should do, the hatred of them was subsiding. Some visitors thought progress was slow. "A year and only this far?" How little did they know of my labours. Marking out metal, hacksawing from the large sheet, filing to correct dimensions and worst of all trying to drill holes in the right places. One small bracket could easily take a whole day. When eventually I had enough brackets to fit the control box, which holds the joystick, some more which allowed the rudder pedals to swivel back and forth, even more to secure floor-boards and those which gripped the tie rods across the fuselage and would be the attachments for wings and undercarriage, I could then put in place the rather basic seat. Sitting in the whole contraption was only done when there was no-one else about. Few things look more silly than a man of mature years perched in a plywood box, setting his jaw against the imaginary elements, and making engine noises. Although I took many photographs of the plane throughout its construction, none show its builder sitting in it until the first engine run. There were perfectly good reasons for clambering aboard, when length of leg dictated the rudder pedal position, where the throttle lever should be placed, which side should the ignition switches be situated so that the propeller swinger would see if they were on or off. It was while working out some of these minor problems that memories from way back flitted across my mind and I was way back to Elementary Flying Training School (EFTS) days.

CHAPTER TWO
You can't be an air-gunner

Southampton's heritage

The Itchen Bridge will take you 'cross the tide
And bring you to the city's Woolston side.
From there you still can see a factory floor,
Where once stood sheds, down to the shore.
There too, the concrete slipway climbs
Up to the level used in former time.
The passing years try hard to hide and fade
This site where history once was made.

There from his office window Mitchell saw
The flashing flight of seagulls, rise and fall.
Did this inspire that genius to make
The streamlined craft, which fought for freedom's sake.
Was it upon that floor, now cracked and worn,
That Britain's air defence was born,
Though often since we've realised how few,
Because of this blessed spot the Spitfire flew.

"You can't be an air-gunner." I was told this, the day after my 18th birthday in January 1941. Three of us, all office boys from firms whose establishments were in the lower part of the town of Southampton known as 'Below Bar'. We had spent our lunch hour striding up to the Lamb Hall, which was 'Above Bar' just beyond the town's shopping centre, and there, within the recruiting office, were prepared to give our voluntary service to king and country as keen-eyed gunners, sitting in the back of Blenheim bombers, as shown in the recent RAF recruiting pamphlets. Our complete lack of any of the required educational qualifications such as School Cert. or Matric. (the school exams of the time - School Cert. was roughly equivalent to the modern GCSE, Matric. to A Level) excluded us from any other aircrew job. Yet, here was this chap saying, "You can't be an air-gunner." After a short pause, long enough for our expressions to register crestfallenness, he continued, "You have to volunteer for aircrew, where you will be classified as a u/t Pilot, a u/t Observer, or a u/t Wop/AG." I faintly wondered which air force a Wop/AG flew for, but said nothing, waiting for more explanations to be revealed. U/t, we were told, meant 'under training'. Pilot and Observer seemed obvious enough. WOP was short for wireless operator, and AG, of course, air-gunner, two jobs for the price of one.

We three lads were all about the same age - Jim, possibly a few months the eldest, Cliff, just a little older than me. In the last eighteen months, from the start of the war, we had watched some of the British Expeditionary Force leave the docks with hundreds of trucks, lorries, tanks and guns, and a brave sight they were. We had cheered regiments of soldiers as they marched through the Southampton High Street, their bands playing them all the way to the troop ships. We had lost a couple of friends who disappeared at Dunkirk. They had only recently been called up into the Militia. We had witnessed our sector of the Battle of Britain being fought above our heads. I had witnessed Flt Lt J.B. Nicholson dogfighting over the town and eventually baling out from his blazing Hurricane, after shooting down his enemy. For this action he was awarded the V.C. His was not the only parachute to descend at that time. I assumed the others were Germans and all coming down above the River Test, quite close to the village of Marchwood. I believe they were all fired at by over-zealous Home Guard rifles, who were taking pot shots at the enemy fighter planes.

Southamptonians, including we three, had suffered the blitz, hiding in shelters when things got too hot, but often braving the bombs to watch the fire brigade's unsuccessful attempts to stop the town from burning down.

So there we were, in the front line, or jolly near to it, with, in my case, only a Home Guard rifle and five bullets to fend off the might of the whole German Army if it ever decided to invade; and we all thought it would. All this, and we three still too young to be let into the war proper.

Back at the Lamb Hall, the man in blue was droning on again.

"Fill up these forms - wait over there - go through there - strip off." It was ever so cold in January. I had been told by old sweats that if you were still warm and could cough, you were 'in'. We coughed and we were in, at least for the moment. Next, in a day or two, to Uxbridge. Fill up more forms - wait over there - strip off; then, after all this, repeat the oath, receive a Bible and so, by then, I was no longer me, I was now just a lengthy un-remember-able number. I must also say, that during that time there were searching interviews before senior-ish RAF Officers, who looked like the service equivalent of Mr Chips, before we were accepted. The service sausage machine turned, and out came Jim, as a u/t Pilot, Cliff as a u/t Wop/AG, and then me, by some stroke of luck, a U/t Pilot. We returned home by train through heavy snow, were diverted from Eastleigh, around to Romsey and Salisbury. That long way round to Southampton's West Station was because of an unexploded bomb somewhere on the down line. Indoors, after I had related my experiences, my mum was bravely pleased, my father said he would have done the same thing if he had been thirty years younger, and my girlfriend was ever so proud and flaunted the brooch I had bought her, of a pair of silver wings. As for me, of course, I was beyond everything with excited anticipation. After all, I always felt I was born to be a pilot.

I still have my earliest memory of being taken to the great Wembley Exhibition of 1924, when I was about eighteen months old and being sat in an aeroplane. At least, I was told I had done so, so I think I can remember it. I can most certainly remember when I was three, sitting on my mum's knee in the front of some old biplane and watching lorries crawling along Wide Lane, way below us as we flew around Atlantic Park at Eastleigh. My father, who was also keen on flying, insisted on getting us, that is my elder brother and I, into the air on as many occasions as possible. How then could I escape what I thought to be my destiny?

A few years on, my brother became an apprentice with the Supermarine Aviation Company, who had built the Schneider Trophy racing sea-planes and was working on the new fighter, later to be named the Spitfire. I was attending night school to try for an apprenticeship in the RAF I'd better say, right now, I didn't make the RAF apprenticeship, I didn't even take the exam, but I won't bore you with my excuses.

A pilot I became. More of that later. ..

Office Boy to Airman.

We hear a lot these days about the 'work ethic', whatever that may mean. Its great moral value means little to me. I suppose, if you haven't got a job, then the great 'work ethic' is probably ongoing or meaningful, or both or neither, depending on which way you view such things.

When I left school, just after my fourteenth birthday, getting a job was number one priority, as it is now, and, as now, hundreds and hundreds of people didn't have one. As I cycled around the Civic Centre on my way to my first interview with a local firm of solicitors, I felt for the crowds of men sitting along the low walls of the Labour Exchange, waiting and waiting. Being out of work in the nineteen-thirties was a much worse prospect than it is now.

My shoes were polished, my bike was polished, my face was polished and a fair smear of solid lavender Brilliantine plastered my hair in place. I located the solicitors' office easily enough, as an enormous brass plate fixed to the massive front door, proclaimed the multi-partnered title. That plate, in its highly polished state, reflected mine. My wait in the waiting-room was short. I was then ushered into the presence of the senior partner. The likeable god sat in his deed-ridden state room. I was followed in by 'Strubell' (we were shouted at by our surnames in those days) who was the chap in charge of the outer office, where I was to be the lowest creature and was to start at 8.30 a.m. on Monday. The interview took little time, mainly I believe, because all office boys employed there came from my elementary school and that school had never sent them a bad one – yet.

Although I left the interview with the smugness of 'I've got a job' snobbishness, I knew at the bottom of my heart, that work, that awful word, was not what I was made for, and, strangely enough, I have been consistent in that belief all my life, so far. I'm not at all sure how I stuck the next four years of fear and boredom. Fear of everyone in authority, which of course everyone was; fear of doing the wrong thing, and often succeeding in that, and fear of being dragged down into the mire of the humdrum existence of office work. Bored because I could never get interested in other people's business, which is the stock in trade of the solicitor, and bored because I craved adventure.

The day war broke out

Yes I remember Sunday September the third
The radio had blurted out the word
'War' - old Chamberlain's sobering voice
Had given us but little choice

Old men in their fifties predicted doom
The country's overcast with gloom
But for me and my pal Pete
We both went dancing in the street

What fun to ditch our dull routine
And take on a more exciting dream
Of guns and bombs and aeroplanes
And exploding ammunition trains

We'd seen it all at the local flicks
With the dirty huns and their dirty tricks
And Errol Flynn and David Niven
Blow the blighters to high heaven

Dawn patrol - I'd watched it twice
To be absolutely precise
I saw myself as a future ace
With me taking Niven's place

So off to the 'Raff' recruiting station
To volunteer to save the nation
To be reprimanded by some three striped rough
To 'Go home sonny - come back when you're old enough.'

The office job - a tiresome bind
The next few months were most unkind
Few bombs and bangs - a phoney war
Life became a prolonged bore

But - of a sudden - the bombing blitz
When half the town was blown to bits
I wondered if this might forecast defeat
So much for the dancing in the street

Time took its ever lumbering course
Time at last to join the force
And become one of the Brylcream blue
In the footsteps of the few

So dancing became part of life
Enjoyment in the midst of strife
Gyrations then - so way up high
Our dance of death was in the sky

Yes I remember that old September date
Was it luck or skill or fate
That still allows we all to meet
Though we've packed up dancing in the street

We now - we crumbling ancient crocks
Watch - Come Dancing - on the box

It's a terrible thing to admit, but on the day old Chamberlain told the nation we were at war, my big worry was that it might be all over before I was old enough to take part. The older types who were in the Great War assured us youngsters that any modern war could never last long, as bombs and gas would bring everything to a swift end, and, anyway, there were so many pacifists in the country that no one would take up arms. The rest of the population would follow Oswald Mosley and would welcome the enemy into England with arms raised in Nazi salutes.

On that very afternoon of the third of September 1939, I chanced to meet, in Regents Park Road, my fellow office boy, who was two years my senior and so held a higher position in the office than I did. He was also the age to be called up and quite looked forward to the adventure. We literally danced for joy for the war which we selfishly thought might break the monotony. I'm not sure whether I should be ashamed, though I later felt sorry for that poor chap who was killed in the Western Desert a few years on. Let's hope he found some of the adventure he wanted, before, for him, it all stopped.

Adventure must be all things to all people, although, I assume it usually centres around the business of discovery and venturing into the unknown. Adventure is something I find difficult to accurately define. Could it be the knight on his white charger, like the 1930's swashbuckling film star, fencing his way through impossible odds; the spy, cloaked and daggered, softly creeping through the darkened streets of some foreign city; or a scientist chasing some remote bug which must be lurking somewhere in the unknown for all of us; the journey through life and even the next journey, after we've moved on from this world?

My adventurous journey started with the arrival of the papers calling me to the Initial Training Wing of the R.A.F, entailing the longest train journey I'd ever been on, from home to some well-known holiday resort in the far west of England. So, in no time, it was goodbye to the hum-drummers at the office, a brave goodbye from Mum, tears from the girlfriend, and assurance from my father that had he been thirty years younger he would have done the same thing.

Throughout my travels, I have always been fascinated by the names of railway stations as they appear through the carriage windows, un-blurring their way to a standstill, till they become readable, then conjuring in my mind geographical or historical places and events to start the imagination racing away, wondering what lies beyond the station platform. How well I can still remember the thrill of seeing Gare du Nord, Paris, Johannesburgh, Delhi, Bulawayo, Brussels, Bombay - Babbacombe.

Babbacombe? That was where I had to get out. Line up, march off, stand still, go there, do that, get this, hold these, fall in, keep in step. I had by now taken an amusing dislike for all corporals with very short haircuts. I'd had my hair cut short, a few days before, in anticipation of service regulations, but still, according to this skin-headed corporal, I qualified for the profession of violinist and not aircrew. Most of those mini-dictators, I'm almost certain, have become our present-day traffic wardens. By the time we were all squeezed into enormous boots. prison-grey shirts, rough blue uniforms, fore and aft hats which only stayed on if you walked with a list to starboard, we had lost all our previous individual identity, although I remember thinking at the time, as I stood in the rear rank of our first parade in full uniform, that we could all fly, Dumbo fashion, by the look of all those ears sticking out from hairless heads.

It is the delight of the sadist to smile when inflicting pain on his victims. How well I found this out, queuing up, the next day, for the ceremonial puncturing of the bodies by the Medical Officers and their orderlies. Needles were jabbing all of us with anti-this, anti-that, blood tests, vaccinations and anything else our pincushion arms could take. I had never been jabbed by any kind of hypodermic before. I was surprised. I was even more surprised to find so many members of this queue, the cream of Britain's youth, fainting and flaking out all over the shrubs and bushes of the medic's garden, while the white-coated orderlies, smiling, urged us onwards.

The very thought of the hypodermic needle still gives me the shudders, even though, some years later, I had a course of penicillin, requiring the use of a rather large diameter needle pushing the early treacle-like mixture into various parts of my torso, at three-hourly intervals, day and night for a week. I should have got used to jabs. I haven't.

After our basic induction at Babbacombe, we moved on to the Trebarwith Hotel in Newquay, our home for the next few weeks, where an assortment of younger RAF Mr Chips tried hard to instil into my unresponsive brain some of the mysteries of mathematics, navigation, gunnery, aircraft recognition, Morse, and, I'm sure, other sundry subjects with above all, RAF Law. This essential subject, most of which completely escapes my memory, included the exact dimensions of deep and shallow latrines, and from some remote section of King's Regulations, the precise distance an airman is allowed to sleep from his horse.

Sometime later, when I was serving in India, one of my duties was to inspect the great Victorian barrack blocks, used originally by red-coated cavalry, where the stables for the horses were part of the structure, and it was very easy to be not more than twenty-five yards from your mount. Those blocks were then housing my unfortunate airmen, in the main buildings and their adjacent stables. It seemed to me that someone had borrowed the K.R's from the army, substituting the word airman for soldier, and not properly revising them for the RAF They had also borrowed the buildings with little revision.

Marching up and down in front of the Newquay hotels, and sometimes in the local car parks, was another essential to train the would-be pilot. Quick march, slow march, halt, stand at this or that, left turn, right turn, about turn, salute everyone or no-one with a one pause twos, longest way up shortest way down. God, where were the aeroplanes? I had done enough of this synchronised walking about while in the Home Guard, and before, as a Sea Cadet. Having tried the uniforms of the Navy and Army, I hoped the RAF would have thought up something better than this infernal marching as a way to instil discipline. No such luck, it was all down to doing what you are told, when you are told to do it. I thought it suppressed personal initiative. At the very least, I felt, we should run around, holding our arms sideways and making engine noises.

A break in this nonsense occurred when we were marched to the stores to receive our flying kit. The amount issued to us was quite fantastic, and, crammed tight, still filled a large kit bag. The flying suit itself was called a 'Sidcot', named after its designer, a famous RAF officer, Sidney Cotton, This was made of thin canvas-like material and shaped like rather roomy overalls, with zip-fasteners for all functions and occasions. It also sported a button-on fur collar. Directly beneath this was worn another and more snug-fitting garment which resembled a dark brown down quilt, again filled with convenient zips and called by most an 'inner'. There were three pairs of gloves, silk, woollen and leather, all worn one on top of another, a vast white pullover, which reached to my knees, fur-lined flying boots and, last of all, a leather helmet and goggles. This was high fashion for the nineteen forties' pilot. Back at the hotel we all dressed up, and after donning the right determined look and heroic stance, took photos of each other. Looking at mine, only the other day, I could hardly believe how naive one could be.

Doug in flying uniform, 1941

One day the great Air Marshal, Sir Trafford Leigh Mallory, blustered along, looking vaguely like a cross between Charles Laughton and Hermann Goering, to inspect us and to ask all in turn what we wanted to fly. I slightly misheard the great man, and said, "Yes, I certainly wanted to fly, the sooner the better." I got it right the second time and managed to give the suppressed answer 'Spitfire'. I was pleased that at least somebody remembered we were going to fly something.

We suffered a contrast a short time later when Sir Archibald Sinclair, the Air Minister, also arrived, and was eased round to meet us. Poor chap looked waxen-faced and worn out. The handshake, after dozens of eager young men, was a wincing paw. Neither of these two 'founts of all knowledge' said where we would be going to learn to fly, although the rumour was that we might well be off to do our elementary flying training in America. The possibilities were, to stay in England, train in Canada, be lucky and go to the U.S.A. or possibly go as far as Southern Rhodesia (now of course called Zimbabwe).

The six weeks of Initial Training were soon over and we were sent on leave; that too was soon over. The next move was to West Kirby, on the Wirral, and this made us feel sure a boat awaited us at Liverpool, but in the dead of night we crept off to Glasgow, boarded the P & 0 ship S.S. *Moultan*, and set sail due west for four or five days, leading an enormous convoy of ships stretching back to the horizon. 'U.S.A, here we come,' I thought. Almost six weeks later we landed at Durban.

I can remember little of the actual place, except that the population turned out in their thousands to carry us off to the highlights of their wonderful town and to give us the time of our lives. After the austerity of England, this was bliss. Cars, and big cars at that, lined the docks, collecting the convoy's complement of troops, thousands of them, including the sixty aircrew trainees. The people of Durban showed us generosity quite unbeknown and unexpected. The same spirit I found in Capetown on my return months later. The three days spent in Durban allowed me to see the film *Gone with the Wind*, after sneaking out of camp and after the curfew imposed upon us servicemen. It also allowed me to get rather merry on 'Ginger squares', that is, brandy and ginger ale, and eating too much at the Playhouse, a wonderful establishment which gave the impression of being a great walled garden, dotted with restaurant furniture, a mass of Indian waiters, serving excellent food and drink, and all the time the whole place kidding you that the stars in the vast ceiling were real.

Off then again by train to Southern Rhodesia. The journey lasted a couple of days, days of magical, changing scenery and even more magical place names on the station platforms. At last to Bulawayo. Conditions for us aircrew were, to say the least, primitive. We were housed in huts, very like the native huts with their thatched roofs and straw sides. The site had been the town's old cattle market. Our sleeping accommodation was shared with all manner of creepy crawlies, who, having been there first, classed us as intruders. Flying ants, mosquitoes and locusts had air superiority, while scorpions, snakes and spiders were our enemy land forces.

Socially, Southern Rhodesia gave the impression of insisting that the Edwardian era had not quite ended. The good ladies in the services clubs in the town of Bulawayo, were like well-bred maiden aunts to us all, putting us on our best behaviour at all times so as not to let the side down.

On Saturday nights, dinner dances at the few hotels were colourful affairs with the young ladies in lovely evening dresses, a habit which was frowned upon in war-torn England. Chaperoned by mums and aunts, the lasses danced only with the chaps within the invited parties, so we soon became adept at moving into the right circles and becoming part of the 'in' set. It was a good way to pass the time of waiting, but not what we were there for. The Battle of Britain was ages ago. When would we ever get our chance, or would the war finish before we were ready? Probably not, at the rate things were going, especially as our army seemed to be going backwards on all fronts, and more especially now that Japan had just beaten hell out of the Americans at Pearl Harbour.

They, the Americans, were still reeling from what they called 'the underhand blow'. I think it was really an under-the-seat blow, having been caught with their trousers down. I imagine the Yanks thought they were sitting pretty in their time-honoured 'non-intervention' state.

Still no aeroplanes for us. It was not until towards the end of the year that I was posted to Salisbury, the capital city (now Harare of course), to the Elementary Flying Training School at Belvedere, where I found my first RAF aeroplane, an open-cockpit Tiger Moth.

CHAPTER THREE
The flying tea chest

I can only think, that having started my flying career with an open cockpit machine, I should revert to the same thing later. The cockpit of my Replica Plans S.E.5a, to give it its full title, was minute. The replica is built to somewhere around 80 per cent of the original, depending from where you measure it. The span is only about eighteen inches less each side. The chord, or width of the wing, is considerably smaller and the height differs by about one and a half feet. Having been scaled down to around the three quarter mark, it really only fits a person of three quarter size. Fortunately, I am one of those; in fact, I'm sure I've shrunk in height over the years, probably due to all the pressures one encounters in life's journey. So, although I fit the cockpit reasonably well, there is certainly no room for a lot of paraphernalia, which so many modern pilots appear to consider necessary to carry around in a "spam can" or up-to-date metal aircraft.

The S.E.5a instrument panel

My cockpit design concentrates on a functional approach more than anything else. I have placed the airspeed indicator top left on the panel, where, with the minimum of eye movement, I can watch the ground and the instrument, when approaching to land. Immediately underneath is the altimeter. Those two flying instruments are the ones I should be using most. The compass, turn and slip, vertical speed indicator are spaced around conveniently, with the engine instruments collected together on the right of the panel. The petrol tap, priming pump and ignition switches are on the right. The switches are outside where they can be seen by the person swinging the propeller. I've made an oversized throttle lever and an oversized friction nut, to stop it slipping. The carburettor hot air lever is just below the throttle and easily get-at-able. This may all sound a bit pedantic, but thinking back to aircraft like the Bristol Blenheim, where nearly all the manual controls were either just out of reach or could not be seen, or when found, took the skin off your knuckles in trying to operate them, then imagine the poor chaps who coped with this, as so many of us did, and all that at night, I think one can see why a workmanlike cockpit is something to be sought after by most older pilots.

The seat presented certain difficulties. My first effort was somewhat reminiscent of an 'old man's club'' leather armchair, very comfortable, very good-looking, but very heavy. Seat Mk11 I had made by a basket-maker from Sedgemoor in the Somerset wetlands. Very light, but not so comfortable. It is difficult to gauge just the right sitting angle for the seat when the fuselage is perched on the bench; consequently, although I believe, with much juggling, I have made it about right for me, when anyone else flies my aeroplane, they will have to re-cushion the thing to suit themselves.

The seat was an essential to get more or less right, so that the position of the rudders was correct for my length of leg. The pedals themselves were designed as open stirrups, which I covered over to avoid my feet slipping right through, remembering the tale of one of my squadron members who did that very thing whilst looping a Hawker Hart. He did not enjoy the antics of the aeroplane and eventually left his loose-fitting flying boot in the bowels of the cockpit in an effort to extricate his foot. He managed a successful landing, albeit with a bit of a hop. It could be said that forever after he suffered with cold feet, but that would be a double exaggeration.

The joystick is made somewhat like the original, with a rounded spade grip, which I find very comfortable and get-holdable. I think the tailoring of the aircraft to one's liking places the stamp of the builder upon it, making it very much one's own thing. All these sophisticated goings-on were going on with the plywood box still in the elementary stages. Raw plywood glared from all angles. I would never have been surprised if someone had stamped 'Ceylon' on the side and filled it with tea-leaves.

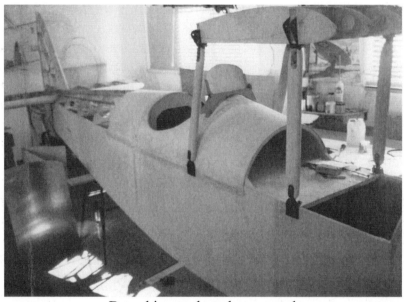

Boxed in, ready to be covered

Time to cover this pale nakedness with, first, a fine fabric called 'madapolam', then colour. To get the madapolam to stay on the surface of the plywood, thinned red dope was scoured and pressed into the fabric and through into the wood. This turned out to be not quite as easy as I had imagined, as the ply is reluctant to absorb any dope until it is lightly sanded to remove an almost varnish-like surface, then the dope is equally obstinate in uniformly spreading itself through the material, which, in turn, insists on forming small blisters when nearly dry.

Liz and I spent short periods of doping and scrubbing with brush and pad, then rushing out of the hangar to gulp fresh air, as the fumes became unbearable. I believe, in the Great War, the girls in the aircraft factory dope shops were expected to spend twenty minutes in the laden atmosphere before a break. They did much better than us.

By the time the complete fuselage, including the turtle deck, was covered and had dried to a blister-less pink colour, and better still, we had relieved headaches with aspirins, the contraption started to take on the same look which I could remember of small machines being built at Southampton's Eastleigh aerodrome, when I used to snoop around there, as a boy.

The smell was also very nostalgic. In those far-off days it was possible to walk around the Eastleigh hangars without any security-minded gents inquiring why you were there, so, living within cycling distance from the field, I spent a lot of my time gazing in awe at various types of flying machines and wishing to become one of those dashing Adonises who, garbed in white overalls, would fly about in Moths or Avians.

Odd-looking flying objects sometimes appeared in the hangars, unlike any real aeroplanes, with the tag of Autogyro. Mr Cierva lived in Southampton; maybe it was his whirling winged efforts. The Kay autogyro was yet another. In fact, an autogyro club was formed and flew at Southampton and Hamble. I remember the talk within my family of it being bound to fail as they flew on Sundays when they should be observing the sacred day of self-enforced boredom.

Occasionally I did fly, as in 1929 when the *Prince Henry*, a Handley Page W8, arrived to give passenger flights. Sitting by the open window opposite the massive uncowled Rolls Royce Eagle engine, was, to say the least, noisy. The passengers' basket chairs were fairly uncomfortable, but the thrill was quite out of this world.

Prince Henry, a Handley-Page W8

A short trip in an Airspeed Courier was another experience. This was one of the first British aircraft to have a retractable undercarriage, which put its speed beyond anything I had so far flown in.

Alan Cobham's circus was an absolute must, and although I was never quite tall enough to always see above the heads of the crowds to watch the flour bombing of the eloping bride, I still have fond memories of those wonderful afternoons.

I should explain. Airshows had to try to entertain all sorts of customer, from those who were dead set on flying in Mr Cobham's ten seater, three engined, Airspeed Ferries, or the more affluent and daring who could afford a few aerobatics in the Moths, to the watchers who had come to enjoy the day out. Consequently, other aerial spectaculars were laid on, one being a slap-stick performance in a good old pantomime tradition of a lad dressed as a bride, flowing tresses, long dress and lots of wooden doll make-up, eloping with her boyfriend in his bull-nosed Morris car, hotly pursued by a shot-gun equipped father in an Avro 504 and bombing the runaways with flour bags. Yet another diversion was the dear old soul persuaded to fly for the first time, being pushed into a biplane, sitting there nervously and even trying to get out as the so-called pilot swung the propeller. Before he, the pilot, was able to run round the wing to take his place in the cockpit, after the engine had started, the old soul was off, protesting violently, as the plane careered down the field, becoming airborne at the, seemingly, most acute and dangerous angles. Erratic flying, by the impersonator, continued until, with spluttering engine, the poor plane executed several extremely bouncing arrivals, the old soul standing up and waving her umbrella most of the time.

Wingwalking, parachuting, formation flying, were all happening to keep the crowds enthralled. The pilots performing all these diversions flew with superb skill. The old adage of 'the show must go on' was very much adhered to, come rain or shine, and, of course, being in the English summer we always had some rain.

By the late thirties Atlantic Park or Eastleigh Aerodrome, or by whatever name it was labelled, became a much more business-like place. No more spending, as I had done years before, the whole day watching two youngish chaps struggle with an R.E.8 whose engine refused to fire on all cylinders, then when all was well to take off, climb to about two thousand feet overhead, for one of the occupants to leap out and parachute down near enough to us for him, on landing, to pass the hat round for the small crowd to show appreciation in a monetary way. Things were changing fast,

After a 'tip-off' from my brother who worked at Supermarine, I arrived one day at my usual spectating point on the western barbed-wire fence, a few yards from the first 1918 wooden hangar. There it was, the most beautiful aeroplane I had ever seen. Beautiful in all respects, a beautiful blue colour, beautiful in shape. I could think of nothing more beautiful. The little numbers on the rear of the fuselage proclaiming 'K5054' have been forever etched in my memory. It was some years later that I flew a Spitfire, but my love for the machine started that day at Eastleigh.

Anyway, back to colour on the S.E.5a. After the red dope, to counteract the effects of ultra-violet or infra-red rays, or both, a coat of silver dope had to be applied; this, to stop heat absorption so I'm told by the experts. Then the final colour. Much research went into trying to find the correct colour which would have been used in World War 1. "Quite simple," I was told, "Protective Colouring No. 10 or P.C.10" - a mixture of yellow ochre and lamp black, which turned out a greenish brown. That sounded reasonable, but contemporary pictures painted in colour made fuselages much greener and less brown. The cardboard model I had made in the thirties required a dark green fuselage and French-grey wings. In the end, I happened to meet a very ancient gentleman who actually worked on these aeroplanes in France. His explanation was that the colours varied, often because whichever dope was available at the time was used. Often, he said, aircraft would arrive from the factories, flown straight to the front line by pilots returning from leave, and could arrive there, more or less primed but unpainted. Certainly, he thought, there was little uniformity.

Squadron markings were another stumbling block. He again came to the rescue, by telling me how, to confuse the enemy and everyone else, squadron markings were often changed, so that all that one reads from books is not necessarily true. That gave me a fair amount of leeway. I decided to do what I thought would look good and ended up with the fuselage a darkish green; the tops of the wings, a brownish grey; underneath the wings, an unbleached calico colour; the roundels, a good strong red, white and blue, and the squadron markings a white bar each side of the roundels. For the serial number of the aircraft I used my old squadron number.

Having said all this, I must explain that no-one is allowed to daub their aircraft with RAF markings and exclude the civil registration letters, without special permission from the Civil Aviation Authority and the Ministry of Defence. In both cases, the letters I received allowing me to do so were most courteous and I am very proud to be able to fly thus adorned.

Using a spray gun for spraying cellulose paint was yet another skill in which I was badly deficient. It always looked so easy when I had watched the experts do it. After much experimentation, using more and more thinners, I seemed to reach a point where, if

I kept the gun moving in the prescribed manner, I gradually built up a layer of colour without the whole lot running down the surface like a mini Niagara. The fuselage, propped on boxes, was wafted, coat after coat, with the dark green colour, markings and roundels all masked off. Also masked, the large letter 'G', my surname initial, on both sides of the fuselage just aft of the roundel and squadron bars. Major James McCudden, the well-known World War 1 ace, favoured a large 'G' on his S.E.5a. Mine was not to copy him, but just for my own identification.

Doug spraying the fuselage

Fortunately, the weather at the time of spraying was nicely warm and dry, allowing me to spray outside in the back garden. I wondered why the grass beneath the wing took on a darker shade of green, until I saw the residue of the paint floating downwards in a mist of cellulose. More paint seemed to colour the grass than ever stuck to the aeroplane.

Miles of masking tape was used to attach newspapers to the pieces which were not to be painted. It's quite surprising how paint can find its way past the slightest unmasked part. Blanking off the roundels took ages, and miles more tape. Circle upon circle of paper had to be cut out and affixed. Red, white, blue, green, grey and off-white, all took their turn to be squirted onto the surfaces. Much carrying in and out, much turning around took place over the time before the last pieces of masking tape were removed and the resplendent wings sat finished in their cradle.

I'll make a comment here. It is most useful, if not an absolute must, to have a wife who will willingly stop what she is doing, and come to the assistance in the lifting, carrying, holding, heaving or anything else connected with the progress of this most important project, and all with enough enthusiasm and encouragement to make one feel that this really is the most worthwhile thing to happen in one's life.

By the way, all that dark green grass turned brown and died.

I have dealt with the paint spraying all in this one short passage as it seemed more appropriate to do so. Actually, the fuselage was sprayed almost exactly a year before the wings, the time in between being taken up with constructing all four wings and this being a lot more complicated than I had imagined.

Within my local LAA Strut (the name given to a LAA district group) was a very 'keen type', who, apart from being in on the design of modern, fast and complicated aeroplanes for a living, launched out in his spare time, into the aircraft wood business. No mean feat this. His expertise in the selecting, cutting and testing with all the very exacting procedures to produce the wood needed for aircraft construction, was fantastic. He it was who delivered to me the most faultless spars for the wings, along with dozens and dozens of other smaller pieces, beautifully cut, planed and labelled.

Hours were then spent drawing out, drilling and jig-sawing the rib webs from one-eighth of an inch plywood. There was a tendency to think that I was only making lots of noise and sawdust, but slowly the racks on the wall were filling up with a vast number of uniform ribs. The wings are made somewhat like a wide ladder, the long side pieces being the spars and holding them apart, or if you prefer it, together, are the ribs. These are made up of a rounded nose section, in this case, seven inches in front of the first spar. Then the centre web of twenty-two inches between the front and rear spars, and behind that a tail piece of eleven inches; the complete chord (the width of the wing) being forty-two inches adding the leading and trailing edges at the extreme ends. All this forms the aerofoil section which gives the essential lift when the wing is dragged through the air.

The rounded wing tips were made from laminated laths of one eighth inch by one inch spruce, which had to bend through ninety degrees in a wide radius. This was achieved by making male and female jigs of chipboard and clamping the glue-covered strips in between. Wood will not naturally take up a ninety degree bend without a certain amount of coaxing. I used the water method of bending. This required the use of the bath with several inches of hot water, allowing the wood to soak for some time, and usually at the time when some member of the family considered they had a greater right to soak. As I made all the laminated tips for wings, tail planes and rudders for Des's aeroplane and my own, the bathroom was forever engaged.

I was surprised how immensely strong the finished laminations became. Planing these boomerang-shaped pieces to their correct thickness presented a problem. Maybe there are ways of holding such shapes onto a bench, so that a wedge-shaped section can be planed satisfactorily. I never found it, and usually ended up with the wood on the floor and me in a very bad temper.

To stop the wing collapsing like a set of parallel rules, drag and anti-drag rods are stretched diagonally from stations where compression struts are mounted. The lower wings have the added complications of having the ailerons attached. These control the banking of the aircraft. In this case they are of the differential type, meaning they will go up but not down, so becoming more effective by cutting out a certain amount of drag.

To speed production of the wing ribs, I made two jigs, so that I could make at least two complete ribs per day. The thirty-eight ribs required, still took a long time. The webs, the centre portion, the nose rib, of heavier ply, and the tail web, were held together in the jig by rib caps gripping all three pieces and leaving gaps for the spars to be slotted in. It all sounds so easy when it is being written down, when in reality the process of fitting all these pieces into a gluey jig with gluey fingers, coupled with the acid smell of the glue hardener stinging the nostrils, makes one think there could be nicer things to do.

Doug working on a wing

Time drags when you are not having fun. I found myself, secretly, sitting in the cockpit of my now green box, a little more often. Building the thing was, to me, only a means to an end. Flying it was to be the ultimate.

Some visitors, after looking at the apparent flimsy structure, thought 'ultimate' or, as my dictionary puts it, 'last, final, beyond which nothing exists', was what would probably happen on its first flight. Fortunately, one visitor, who was a light aircraft designer, considered it to be 'built like a battleship'. I wondered if he was referring to the 'Wooden Walls of England'. I think what worried most people was that, when they had studied the 'tea chest' fuselage, they could not see how it was going to support two hundred and thirty pounds weight of engine, plus over a hundred pounds of fuel, plus one hundred and seventy pounds of pilot. I began to have doubts myself, so consoled myself with the thought that, really, that great heavy engine had a nice lightweight fuselage bolted on to it, and that all would be well, especially if I could develop a technique of flying with my fingers crossed, apart from losing a bit of weight.

The engine, an American Continental C90, was one which I had purchased right at the beginning of the project. Completely unlike any engine that was fitted to the original S.E.5a aeroplanes, this one would suit this size of airframe and be a great deal more reliable than the ones of the Great War era. I had spent a fair amount of time stripping this engine to its last nut and bolt, checking all parts and renewing anything that appeared worn or broken. I was surprised at the simplicity of its design compared with the modern car engine. Not having a gearbox makes any engine less complicated; also dispensing with the electrics, starter, generator and battery, saved work and weight. Having satisfied myself that all was well, I reassembled the lower half of the engine, called in a co-operative 'D' licence engineer to check my work, and continued until all was back together, and I hoped serviceable. It had to wait for quite a long time before its first test run, so it sat, rather dejectedly, in the hangar corner covered with sheets.

CHAPTER FOUR

Learning to fly – Tigers

Rhodesia was condemned by the great Sir Alan Cobham as being unsuitable for flying training, due to the altitude of the country, coupled with the turbulent atmosphere produced by lots of sun on lots of scrubland. The R.A.F's answer was to ignore the altitude and the effect it had on reducing the power of our aero-engines, and to fly in the coolest part of the day - very early in the morning. At the absolute crack of dawn, if not just before, we poor sprogs were rousted from our beds. A quick wash and shave, then dash to the antiquated cook-house, where the large cooking hot plates were being warmed up for the day's incinerations. The idea then was to throw slices of bread onto those blackened plates, wait until the bread started to show the same colour, grab it off, smear margarine onto the burning biscuit, wash it all down with a mess tin of over-sweetened tea, and consider that to be how all would-be pilots should start their days.

The course, all thirty of us, would form into ranks and march the couple of miles to the flights. The very first of the morning excursions was chilly. Just cold enough for us, who were wearing shorts, to feel uncomfortable. Uncomfortableness, mixed with anticipation and a stab of fear of the unknown. Many more times in the future would I have that same sensation.

As we neared the aerodrome, the engines of the Tiger Moths could be heard running up in preparation for the morning's flying, The fitters and riggers must have started work even before we had.

Then the first sight of a Tiger, charging towards us, lifting over our perimeter road, then, above our heads, clattering away, gaining height. I got out of step, blundered into the chap in front, walked backwards for a few steps, still following the disappearing aeroplane. 'This is it,' I thought. 'This will be where I show them what it means to be a born pilot.'

At the crew room we were told to don our Sidcot suits, then read the list of the instructors and their pupils. Under the name of P/O Bentley were two others and then my name. "You've got old Bentley," smirked an old-timer from the previous course, who was trying to make up a few flying hours he'd missed in the past week. "I pity you, he always fails two out of his three."

Ten minutes later 'Old Bentley' appeared. He was of medium height, heavy, scowling, his black moustache turned down at the corners. He gave the general impression of having had a good evening and a bad night, radiating loathing to everyone, especially unknown pupils.

"I say, you lad, go and get into No. 64570." That was me he was referring to. My voice squeaked a "Yes, sir," as I gathered up my parachute, dropped my helmet a couple of times, mislaid my gloves, staggered out towards the line of Tigers and hunted for the number. I must have taken ages girding myself with my parachute, putting my helmet on so that the Gosport tubes were in front, fumbling with gloves only to find I had to remove them before I could do up the parachute straps. By then I felt like a cripple or a half-trussed chicken and, worse still, I had to somehow climb into the back seat of the plane. Fortunately, a rigger was alongside, and he pushed and prodded till I was in. Then the straps of the safety harness were draped over my shoulders and hitched to the ones from the floor, and, if only I could find where my Gosport tubes plugged in, I supposed, I was ready. The Gosport tubes were our method of communication between pupil and instructor, being double tubes, one to each ear in the helmet, going to a mouth-piece sticking out in front of the instructor and the same thing going in the other direction.

I was not unaccustomed to speaking tubes, as I had used them in the solicitor's office where I had been an office boy for four years, during which time I could count, on the fingers of one hand, the number of times I had heard and understood what anyone was saying. There, the tubes connected the senior partners' offices with the outer office, as it was called, where we underlings worked in Dickensian squalor. At a puff from the almighty gods, a whistle blew in our office, which had to be quickly answered, otherwise a second blow from above would result in a blast of stale tobacco or the smell of a recent swig of whisky, depending which partner wished to communicate. The message was then shouted down to us. Trying to decipher the burblings mingled with the clatter of ancient Remington type-writers was always beyond me.

Very little time was allowed for me to gather my thoughts as 'Old Bentley' had somehow managed to climb into the front cockpit, get strapped in and be sitting like an impatient Buddha, before I realised he had even arrived. The 'erk' swung the propeller, strange signs were made between 'O.B.' and the erk, strange words were bandied about, the engine started, the wheel chocks were pulled away, so that the Tiger Moth, O.B. and I were trundling out for my first experience in an RAF aeroplane.

Up to now no-one had spoken. This silence was broken by old posh-voiced Bentley saying, "Keep your feet on the floor and keep your hands to yourself until I tell you differently." I heard every word and obeyed. Into wind we turned, off down the field we ran, into the air we climbed. Climb, turn, climb again. This was my idea of bliss, being flown around this uncluttered countryside on a beautiful blue-skied morning. Not for long. The voice from the front said, "Now, place your feet on the rudder pedals and now hold the stick with your right hand. Let the aeroplane fly straight and level." The aeroplane flew itself. Even after this first air experience exercise, the Tiger made a better job of flying itself than with my interference. This was going to be easy.

A Tiger Moth

Afternoons at the Elementary Flying Training School (E.F.T.S) were spent in the classrooms, or at some kind of physical pursuit. Neither of these pastimes appealed to me. Unlike most of my colleagues, I had left school four years ago and had lost the knack of seeing time-tables for classes as a way of life. They, on the other hand, had just left their public schools where carrying a bundle of books from place to place, sitting and absorbing knowledge, trotting out the correct answers in tests of various kinds, was quite second nature. They were mostly splendid people to know, helping me through some more mathematical mysteries and navigational problems.

It must have been lesson two with 'O.B.' when I was introduced to the throttle, then taxiing, and then the great moment, take-off. I couldn't believe what this mad machine was trying to do. So far it had been so nice. Why now must it decide to career across the field at forty-five degrees from the way I'd started? Buddha was not pleased. He was not pleased again and again, as time after time I battled with the rudder in an endeavour to stop the hectic zigzagging. The actual flying around the circuit was getting better, turns were more consistent, the climb, more or less steady, the approach straight, then bang, or bump, or swing, or topple drunkenly from one wheel to the other. No wonder 'O.B.' looked so morose, and all this in his special Tiger which, unlike all the yellow painted trainers, was entirely camouflaged in green and brown.

His pride and joy was being ill-used by me and he didn't like it. Of course, when he demonstrated how it should be done, his Tiger knew he was flying it, and dared not put a foot wrong. 'O.B's' two other pupils suffered the same fate; that Tiger flew for one man only, I was quite convinced.

One morning a few days later, sitting as ready as I ever could be, the call came from the crew-room door. "I say, lad, get into No. 6131." Off I went, this time into one of those all yellow machines, and eventually, out we taxied. Take-off - not too bad, it actually kept straight, circuit - better, approach OK, then the voice from the front, "I've got her." I released control immediately, thinking I had made some error. The Tiger in the hands of the master, swung violently left and looking down to the right, there, three hundred feet below me, crashed, battered and upside down was 'O.B's' pride and joy, the camouflaged Tiger. Some pupil from the last course, flying solo, and trying to amass the hours, had managed to do this dreadful thing. Buddha landed our aeroplane this time. When firmly on the ground, he kicked once or twice at the rudder pedals and then with great control sat 'Buddha-like' and serene, while I taxied in. I realised I was sitting behind a great chap and I felt extremely sorry for him, but, of course was quite unable to tell him so.

The Bustard Flying Club's Tiger Moth

My flying hours were mounting up. The grinding, binding circuits and bumps continued, time after time, round and round. I supposed I must have been getting better. The take-off stayed straighter, the landings were, at times, less bumpy, but I was worried. Each day smug pupils strutted into the mess, casually remarking that they had 'gone solo' that morning, and it was 'a piece of cake'. Some unfortunates crept around, literally in tears, with failure engraved into their dull eyes. I was getting very worried.

P/O Bentley, at the invitation of his pupils, spent a social evening with us in our bar. He eased a little after a quantity of free beer, told us about his days at Old Sarum (near Salisbury) flying Lysanders, and gently probed into our pasts. I suppose I had confided to him that flying was the only thing which made my life worthwhile, because during a quieter moment he became quite fatherly, telling me to be less tense, to try getting drunk at the weekend and above all, not to worry. Undoubtedly that was a turning point, although I didn't know it at the time.

After the weekend, during which I did not get drunk, but did manage to relax, I started the dreaded circuits and bumps again on the Monday with slightly more confidence." By the late afternoon I was to fly with a different instructor, for him to assess my readiness for 'going solo'. P/O Brown, the instructor who was to check me, was known as, and certainly was, the 'perfect gentleman'. All pupils hoped to be on his list. Everyone knew of his reputation of being the most kind, understanding and helpful person, and now, thank God, he was to do my check. If I could successfully fly a couple of circuits without frightening him and generally doing all the right things, he would step out, and off I'd go on my own. This was it.

"Carry on and don't mind me," was all I heard from the front cockpit. Start up, chocks away, taxi out, swing the nose, keep a good look-out, turn into wind, open the throttle and off we go. Wonderful, I actually kept straight. The circuit was flown, as per book, and all was going well. I picked my landing spot when decreasing height across wind, turned onto the final approach and flew straight into the brightest glare of the low sun that I had ever encountered. I was blinded. Good, decent and kind P/O Brown acted at once, dragging out his spotless white handkerchief, then with both hands trying to make a sun visor to shield the light. The sunshine remained unshielded, but the ground disappeared and I, in desperation, bellowed through the Gosports, "I can't see." "All right, I have her," came the calming voice of P/O Brown. He took over the controls and demonstrated his usual perfect landing. I had failed.

Despondency set in and I spent one of the most miserable nights of my life. My flying hours had now passed the total where many of the course had soloed and considered they were on the road to success. The next morning, I again sat in the crew room wondering what, if anything, would happen. 'O.B.'s' face appeared around the door. He looked as if he had had as bad a night as I had. "I say, get into No. 8009," he called. I sheepishly obeyed, and once again went through all the processes of getting a Tiger Moth into the air. I flew a fairly mediocre circuit, still cursing the pathetic performance of the evening before. "Taxi in, please," came from the front and, after we had got back to the lines of aircraft, he spoke again, "Keep the engine running." I did. He, surprisingly, leaped out from the front cockpit, removed his parachute, connected the front harness straps together and with a very casual voice said, "Go and do one circuit," turned away and, without looking at me, disappeared into the crew room. My emotions were so mixed up I could only mutter my usual dry-throated, "Yes, Sir."

My taxiing was just that little bit slower. I very carefully turned into wind and started the take-off run. The Tiger rose from the ground earlier than I had anticipated, due to the lack of bulk in the front, even though I still felt 'O.B.' was there. I realised he wasn't when I found I could see directly forward, a thing that, so far, I'd been unable to do, because of the great leather-clad dome of 'O.B's' head. I was liking this, even feeling confident. Then the realisation hit me, I had to get this thing down again. I suppose I started praying on the down-wind leg of the circuit, till I remembered that God helps those who help themselves, so with a last 'Into thy hands, Oh Lord', I swung into wind, judged the approach just right and, thank God, made quite a good landing. I was hoping all the way round the circuit that 'O.B.' was not watching. After the landing I was hoping he was. I never found out one way or the other. He certainly didn't rush out to congratulate me, neither did anyone else, until my smugness in the mess indicated that I had managed the first small step to becoming a pilot. This happened on the 23rd December 1941. It was the best present I'd ever had, thanks mainly to 'O.B.'

CHAPTER FIVE
The dream takes shape

Undercarriages for aircraft have been a difficulty from the beginning of things. Maybe the Wright Brothers had a good idea with rails, rollers and skids. The proposed supersonic passenger carrier 'Hotol' looks as if it could go back to that sort of thing. The Spitfire, a superb aeroplane in the air, but with an awfully narrow undercarriage, designed by a seaplane expert, gave all of us troubles. The Stirling bomber had an unbelievably long undercarriage which made it look rather like an electric flamingo; again this aeroplane came from a long line of flying-boats, so had little evolutionary undercarriage design experience. Some undercarriages retract, some don't, some don't when they should, some won't come down when they should, and some like my S.E.5a are fixed.

The first S.E.s of 1917 had steel-tubed undercarriages, which gave a great deal of trouble, probably because of the makeshift aerodromes in France with their bumpy surfaces. Later, wood and metal structures were made and, later still, wood only. Which was the most successful and why, I know not. I used the alternative design on the plans, in wood, for my S.E.5a.

After much searching, I came across a knowledgeable chap, a wheelwright by trade, who kept a small supply of well-seasoned and selected ash. Whether he couldn't bear to part with his precious wood - after all, he had had it long enough for it to become part of the family - or whether he was just very, very slow in getting around to business, I'll never know, but it took weeks of waiting, and screaming, to get him to cut the shapes and plane the pieces to what I had ordered. It was O.K. when I got it and I suppose even more seasoned. Ash is a little heavier than the spruce, as per plan, but I thought, much stronger with a lot more spring in it.

A long time was spent splicing the front and back legs together to form the 'V' of the undercarriage. Where the two legs joined, a block fillet neatens the whole thing. Much planing and sanding followed. When the two sets of legs were completed and then varnished, the grain shone out and looked wonderful. Then, of course, more brackets. Wood joined to wood, or wood joined to metal, or anything else which needed joining, seemed to require brackets. Bluing the metal sheet, accurately drawing out the shape, hacksawing it from the large sheet, filing to the scribed line and then drilling the holes, I hoped, in the right places, took many hours. I was never in the best frame of mind after a bracket session, especially after bending them. Bending metal still seems a bit of a hit-or-miss situation. The bender mounted on the bench appeared a very straightforward piece of apparatus. Why it refused to work for me I cannot imagine, unless my aged faculties are on the way out.

Nevertheless, with all the brackets attached and the axle spacers between the wooden legs, it did actually fit onto the fuselage. The axle itself was made with two hefty stubs of thick tube ground to a very smooth surface to take the wheel's oil-lite bearings. The stubs are then held apart by a thinner tube, which stretches across the width of the undercarriage. Very early on this tube started to bend, so I reinforced it with another pushed inside. Also, welded onto the axle are the flanges, which hold the wheel brakes. Brakes were never fitted onto the old S.E.s. My plans required them to be fitted because, being Canadian plans, this design has a tail wheel, as over there all aerodromes have hard runways. Brakes are then an essential. I have fitted a tail skid to my version with the intention of flying from grass fields only, but retaining brakes as they aid turning on the ground. The hubs I used came from a small motorcycle. Small it was, but heavy. The hubs are also heavy. Even after turning a few lumps off and filing out a few holes, they are still heavy.

To get the wheels to look the right scale, I used a sixteen-inch rim. A local expert built up the wheels using robust spokes, the type used for hefty sports cars. At the back of my mind I had visions of some of my landings, which at times make contact with mother earth in a very positive way, and I have been known to arrive three times in one landing. Strength in the wheels and undercarriage could well be essential.

The 1918-style aircraft tyre would have been smooth and

treadles. To get this effect nowadays is almost impossible, although I have seen some tyres made to look authentic by skimming off the tread of a modern tyre, but it leaves very little rubber above the canvas. I compromised by using a ribbed tyre, as used on the front wheel of a motor-cycle. It was my luck to choose something which apparently did not exist; at least, that was what many tyre distributors insisted. The right ones eventually came from Taiwan through an enterprising person who knew what he was on about.

Before I completed the whole assembly, the wheels were given fabric discs. The inside of the wheel was flat and just required the fabric to be stretched from the outside of the rim to the brake drum. The outside of the wheel had to look like the slightly conical shape of the old timers. Their wheels had the spokes attached to the outside of the wheel rim, so that the spokes showed their pattern through the fabric. To achieve that look meant inserting plywood strips from hub to rim, so that the fabric would stretch itself over to give the impression of it being a First World War wheel. It looked quite good when finished and painted. It was a great blessing to have the fuselage on wheels at last. I could trundle the fuselage, inch by inch, across the workshop to give sufficient room to be able to fit the engine.

The engine-bearer had been bolted to the firewall for about two years. It looked like a set of modern coat-hooks and was often used for that purpose. At last it was being put to its proper use. The Lord engine mounts were a trifle expensive for what they were, the bolts through them even worse. I was slowly getting used to the fact that everything attached to the aircraft industry costs the earth. Thank heavens I was not building a modern fighter.

As in all aircraft with engines in front, a firewall is placed between the engine compartment and everything else behind. In this case the petrol tank is directly behind the firewall and over the pilot's legs and feet. My firewall consists of the half-inch thick ply bulkhead covered with an asbestos-backed tin foil, between a sheet of galvanised steel. The engine bearer holds it all together. As few holes as possible are made through the firewall, for obvious reasons. The largest hole, almost an inch and a half in diameter, brought about a lot of heart searching before I could bring myself to drill it. It was there to allow warm air to enter the cockpit around where my feet touch the rudder pedals. As I intended to fly all the year round and could remember the icy blasts up my trouser legs when flying Tiger Moths in the winter, I felt it was a must.

Another hole, a little bigger than I had wished, was for the revolution counter drive to come, straight as possible, from the instrument panel to the back of the engine, passing through the middle of the petrol tank on its way. Ignition switch leads, oil pressure pipes, petrol pipes and temperature gauge pipes only made very small holes, and most of those were on the extreme edges of the firewall, leaving the wall itself to form a good solid barrier between a fifteen-gallon tank of petrol and the hot engine.

The tank was designed to fit into a finger-trapping hole and to me appeared an almost impossible shape to make. My effort turned out to be rather like a misshapen tin plate Dorothy Bag, which fitted very badly and, worse still, leaked. In despair, I cried for help to my brother, who, after all, being in an aircraft factory for half his life and recently a works manager, should know about these things. He, as usual, could see no difficulty, or where any difficulties could arise, and, dismissing me as being my usual stupid self, and one who, following the old adage, 'couldn't do, so he had to teach', set about the job and produced a beautiful tank in no time. I threw my effort on the dump.

I had to face it. Now that the fuselage was on its wheels, the firewall and bearers were in position, the two hundred and thirty pounds of engine had to go on. Some struggle it turned out to be. My shed, cum hangar, was big; at least, it appeared big when I started building; now it was not quite big enough, in fact it was too small. By putting the tail end of the rudderless fuselage right up into one corner and facing it out from there at an angle of thirty degrees, I could just about get the scaffold tower into position. The scaffold tower looked to be about the strongest structure we had to support the engine, and at the same time give us room to move about. A large baulk of wood placed across the top of the tower held the three-pulley winch, whose hook then dangled somewhere near where the engine was sitting on the floor looking defiant. I'm sure these hoists are wonderful gadgets, just as the blurb says, but they do have a knack of stopping all circulation in one's fingers when the thin cords become wrapped round in an endeavour to pull hard. Slowly the weight was taken and the engine rose from the floor, Des doing most of the pulling.

The engine in position

Eventually the whole thing was sufficiently high for the bolts and rubber mounts to be inserted. Not until all four were positioned and the nuts tightened a little, did we relax on the hoist. Surprisingly, the engine just sat there. The bearer didn't pull itself out of the fuselage, the undercarriage didn't collapse; in fact, the engine looked quite happy sitting there in its proper place and almost asking to be run. Quite a long time elapsed before it was run, this being only the first fitting. From now on, or at least all the time the engine was on the aeroplane, I had to crawl underneath to get from one side to the other.

I could just stand in front to turn the engine over, using a plank of wood to act as a propeller, to check for oil leaks. Frantic turning was needed to make any impression on the gauge. I could then check for leaks around the filter, temperature gauge, oil pressure gauge, or anywhere else from which oil could squeeze out. Not until much later did I find the rocker box leaked like mad, and that was during the first engine run. I could, and did, when no-one was looking, sit in the cockpit to see how far away the front of the aeroplane would be and whether I would have any forward visibility with the mass of engine sticking up into view. How different from the absolutely unlimited forward visibility I had from the cockpit of the Beaufighter.

CHAPTER SIX
Advanced Training – Harvards

Musing once more, I recalled how terribly ignorant I must have been regarding the workings of the internal combustion engine when I was at my E.F.T.S. Lectures. The theory of engines and their various systems meant little when it was all in diagrammatic form and no real bits to handle. Keeping all of us fledglings slightly ignorant may have been a good thing; after all, there's not a lot that can be done if an engine needs repair whilst flying. Fortunately, and probably because of the high standard of maintenance, I had never had any engine trouble throughout all my flying training. We were taught how to execute forced landings if all in the front went quiet. We also used to practise restarting the engine in flight. The hardest part of that exercise was to get it to stop. This was done by bringing the nose of the Tiger slowly up, allowing the speed to drop off almost to the stall, keeping well throttled back and turning the aircraft towards the rotation of the prop. If the ignition was switched off, sometimes the propeller would come to a stop. Then the best part. Diving at what appeared to be vertical, switching on again, and at the bottom of the dive, at the pull-out, the propeller should start wind-milling and the noise start again.

Very occasionally nothing happened. Our instructors were clever enough to anticipate this and always demonstrated these manoeuvres above a small satellite landing ground, where it was safe to land, re-swing the prop and take off again.

'O.B.' had by now 'scrubbed' some of his work load of pupils. I still remained. Not, as I had imagined, as the greatest star that had ever flown into his life, but probably not more than average pilot, whom he was willing to put up with. He was absolutely thorough in his teaching, no short cuts, no cutting corners and no short measures of any sort. I realised at the time that this was the only way and that it would stand me in good stead in the future. I was almost beginning to like 'O.B.'. I had always had the greatest respect for him.

Then, of all things, he left to go back to England; and me, only three quarters of the way through the course. For a day or two nothing happened and I could see that my flying hours were falling behind the rest. All was saved eventually by the arrival of P/O Newton. He had just completed a long stint, flying Gladiators and Hurricanes in and around the Western Desert in North Africa. He had, I suppose, been given an instructor's course, arrived at Belvedere and I was to be his first pupil. He appeared to be completely mad and probably was. He thought the Tiger Moth was a tame edition of a Hurricane, and that his first pupil must learn fighter tactics from the word go. I loved it. We spent a considerable time learning aerobatics, stringing the manoeuvres together, starting with a spin, recovering and into a loop, into another and roll off the top, then slow rolling. By then I had lost so much height, I could do no more, but that gave the excuse to low fly, strafing imaginary targets. Once while beating up the flare path just prior to night flying, he misjudged the height and struck the ground with a bit of a bump. Nothing serious, but he said that he had done that once before, hitting the Mediterranean whilst flying a Gladiator in pursuit of some Italian, and in future must be more careful.

His love of aerobatics knew no bounds, but nearly came to an abrupt halt the day he demonstrated a slow roll, but had omitted to strap himself in tightly enough. The first thing I saw, after we had become inverted, was P/O Newton from about the waist up obliterating my view forward. He, still grasping the Gosport mouth-piece, was shouting, "Get the thing back." I did, and he sank back into his seat, considering the whole episode as a great laugh.

Where 'O.B.'" had been the perfect instructor to teach the rudiments of flying, P/O Newton started to show me what fighting was all about. I just couldn't get to the Service Flying Training School fast enough, to fly their smart-looking Harvards.

Belvedere camp was situated on the outskirts of Salisbury, only a short walk to the centre of town. If we had not been required to rise so early in the mornings, we might have had a more interesting social life. As it was, we would occasionally, usually at week-ends, grace the town with our presence to attend the dinner dances at the Grand or Meikles Hotels. Young lady partners were discovered at the South African Christian Society (S.A.C.S.) House, a place rather like a posh Y.W.C.A. The dances themselves were rather glittering affairs, with excellent food and the lasses in colourful evening dresses. Just occasionally, I had a slight feeling of guilt, remembering the rationing and the blackout and the war which I had left back home. When I felt really bad, I'd pack up a food parcel and send it home just to salve my conscience. Jim, one of the office boys I had joined up with, had arrived at another E.F.T.S. a few miles further outside Salisbury, and at these weekend dances, often met us to make a foursome with a couple of S.A.C.S. House girls. His progress on Tiger Moths was even slower than mine and I wondered if he would complete the course.

Cranbourne, the Service Flying Training School, was about five miles the other side of Salisbury. We arrived there with the exalted rank of acting Sergeants, having been promoted from Leading Aircraftmen after the completion of our elementary flying training. This brought in a few more shillings a week to spend in our spare moments.

'Pockets' Cafe', in the main street of Salisbury, was a wonderful place for afternoon tea, cream cakes and brandy snaps. It was whilst walking towards the place, pushing my young lady's bicycle, which I thought the gallant thing to do, and being engrossed in conversation with her, that I accidentally managed to pass, without noticing, a penguin. 'Penguin' was the rather unfair name given to RAF Officers who had no wings, i.e. were not pilots, therefore considered by us to be able to flap but not fly. This hero called after me to stop, then inquiring whether it was my practice not to salute officers, "Salute me now," he demanded. I did, of course, but it is very difficult to look as if you mean it, if in one hand you still have a bicycle.

Some time later, now being over watchful, I spied a brace of penguins advancing. On this occasion, no bicycle, but I was wearing my ridiculous solar topee. This hat had the tendency to make me look as if I was hiding under the dome of St. Paul's.

Nevertheless, a very smart salute was initiated when a couple of steps away. Unfortunately, bringing my hand down from a great height, I struck the peak of the topee, bringing it over my eyes and obscuring the view. The next thing I knew was tripping over the on-coming pavement and landing in a heap in the gutter. From then on, I considered saluting was something to be taken lightly, and later, when I was the one to be saluted, I usually passed the time of day or at least smiled. Pomposity didn't seem to suit me.

Harvards on the airfield in South Rhodesia

The Harvard was a splendid aeroplane. The difference between it and the Tiger Moth was beyond everything. These were big and powerful and metallic and fast and complicated. The cockpit check, which we were obliged to narrate to our instructors, whilst taxiing to the take-off point, was like a Shakespearean script, poetic, but very long. Being perched up in the glass-house of a cockpit was confidence-making to a great degree. Over-confident-making at times and a number of chaps on the course came very bad croppers, taking chances while low flying. Low flying is so good and such fun, that, however many times one is forbidden to do it, it can never not be indulged in. Of course it was dangerous.

My answer was to practise it as much as possible, to become more proficient, hence less dangerous. I still do.

F/O Randrup, my instructor, was probably the best pilot I have ever flown with. After the war, I believe, he became a test pilot for a light aircraft firm, giving superb sales exhibitions. Like 'O.B.' he was a stickler for precision flying, and would rage and storm if I gained or lost a hundred feet in height on the circuit. His greatest insult was to tell me I was flying like a Greek. We had a course of Greeks on the station, who, apart from dressing in rather non-uniform clothing, often appeared wearing hair nets and holding hands with their mates.

His flying was always perfectly executed, although at times frightening, especially on one occasion when he wished to alert a friend of his who lived way out in the bundu. We approached the isolated house at a great speed, then, at just above tree-top height, or so it looked to me, slow rolled half a dozen times while circling the establishment. It awoke the occupant, who came out waving, thinking, like me, that the end of the world was near.

Doug and friend beside a Harvard at Cranbourne

The Harvard course was in two halves - the first, to teach us how to fly the machine; the second, how to use the aeroplane as a weapon.

We started off again with the endless circuits and bumps. Pilots of modern tricycle undercarriage aircraft do not know how the old tail-draggers could swing, especially on landing. All do it, some more than others. I suppose it's to do with lack of keel surface, blanking off the rudder, gyroscopic effect of the prop, torque, or anything else that happens to be about at the time. The Harvard had a fairly vicious swing if not watched. It always happened, as with so many, just when you felt you had made a good arrival and it was all over bar the shouting. Then, just when the concentration lapsed, off it would go trying to ground loop itself around one wheel.

The Harvard was not such an easy aircraft to fly after the dear old Tiger. It was vastly more complicated, with retractable undercarriage, flaps, mixture controls, variable pitch airscrew, wobble pumps, hydraulic systems, electrical systems, emergency systems and a hundred and one other things to watch and remember. Many accidents were brought about by forgetfulness and many by the inability of pupils to appreciate their own shortcomings, coupled with the limitations imposed by the aeroplane. Every single night on which my course flew, some accident occurred, mostly minor ones, but the odd fatality. Two of our Saturday night gang killed themselves by flying low enough to hit the ground. I saw the scar on the brown parched earth and later, the remains of the Harvard. A very sobering sight. I was convinced that low flying must be done with full concentration on the flying and not on the girlfriend waving from the ground.

It was about this time that poor old Jim landed his Tiger Moth upside down. He was physically O.K. but I could see quite plainly that he was never going to make the grade if he progressed to Harvards. He could see it too, and asked to be sent to East London in the Cape, to retrain as the air-gunner he had originally intended to be. By the time I had finished my courses in Rhodesia, he was back in England, as an air gunner in the tail turret of a Wellington bomber.

In the second half of the Harvard course we were expected to be able to fly without too much supervision from the rear seat. A good deal of the time was spent in formation flying, air gunnery, dive bombing, cross country and general fighter tactics. We were told we were going to be posted to Hurricane squadrons in the Western Desert. It's funny how all the best-laid plans and all that, can change in a trice. Change they did. Back in England, Air Marshall (Bomber) Harris had won his argument that bombing Germany with enough tonnage could bring the war to a speedier end. His thousand bomber raid on Cologne had shown just what could be done if enough weight of bombs fell somewhere near the target, which they would with saturation bombing. This meant lots and lots of bombers driven by lots and lots of bomber pilots. We, much to our horror, were to be some of them.

Doug in an Oxford at Bulawayo

We were packed off to an aerodrome near Bulawayo for a quick conversion onto twin-engined Oxford aircraft and then to be sent home to England and Bomber Command. In an overconfident and belligerent mood, we attacked the conversion, determined to fly the Oxford as we had the Harvard. None of this controlled, straight and level, bomber stuff for us. I found the stall turn in the twin-engined aeroplane frightening, and my curving approaches were frowned upon. Low flying was even better as, with no great engine to obscure the view, I could get even lower and see all the things to be avoided.

We must have been a tiresome bunch, and I can only assume that the good, hard-working instructors were very pleased to see us go. I finished the course with a strong recommendation from my instructor to be returned to single-engined fighters.

The highlight of the course came right at the end - the Wings Parade. Only a simple affair, with us survivors lined up before a card table on which was a box of badges. Names were called out by the Station Warrant Officer. We trooped up, saluted the Group Captain, who shook hands with us, then handed over the coveted pair of silver-coloured wings.

Wings Parade, Bulawayo 1942

It's probably only after you get them that you start to earn them. Maybe that's not quite true; you are not given them for nothing. I was, and still am, immensely proud to wear the RAF Wings. The station photographer took pictures of us as we accepted the badges and that was about that. We sewed them on to our jackets after the parade, being superstitiously afraid to do so before, just in case something horrible happened to stop us receiving them. The then-current American films portrayed the same parade for their air force pilots in a very different way, usually with parents and sobbing girlfriends watching, brass bands blaring, screaming formations of aircraft flying overhead and some veteran film star blabbing on about the 'call of duty' and by now, nearly always getting in a mention of Pearl Harbour. We in the cinema always roared with derisive delight.

The journey from Rhodesia via Cape Town, then aboard the *Warwick Castle* to Glasgow, was uneventful, I was glad to say. Travelling alone, being too fast to stay in convoy, the *Warwick Castle* pounded its way into northern latitudes. Because of the shortage of naval personnel, we aircrew were asked to man the guns. I sat, four hours on, then four off, at a gun station up by the squat funnel for the whole of the eighteen day journey. Little did anyone realise that I knew practically nothing about the workings of a Lewis gun, yet there I was, supposedly guarding the ship from aerial attack.

At least I know a bit more about the Lewis gun now, because my S.E.5a has a scale model of a Lewis gun mounted to the top of the centre section. The full size S.E.5a carried two guns, a Vickers protruding from the fuselage with the breech get-at-able from the cockpit, and the Lewis gun above the pilot on a Foster mounting, which was supposed to allow the pilot to change the magazine by sliding the gun down for him to reach it, and all the while still trying to fly it.

Before making the three-quarter sized replicas, a deal of research was gone into. The Imperial War Museum had lots of helpful pictures, and a visit to the Infantry Weapons Museum at Warminster was of great help. There, they have just about all the information required, with an extremely helpful team of gentlemen who knew all there was to know about weaponry. I was surprised how authentic my guns looked, when made. Guns have to have gun sights: the Vickers, a ring and bead, the Lewis an Aldis, which is like a small telescope. All these fitments certainly add a great deal of character to the look of my aeroplane. Guns, in general, do not appeal to me. They look spiteful and make a lot of noise. I can never fathom the fascination many people have to own them. My wooden ones are as near as I want to get to guns these days.

During my many courses in Training Command, machine-guns played a large part of the armament teaching. All N.C.O. instructors must, I believe, have been trained by the same man using the same manual, as their patter was identical. Even the staccato delivery of their speech was identical. What they were on about I could rarely follow, but I can recall their parrot-like phrases concerning, quote, "The bullet nips smartly up the barrel, hotly pursued by the gases," and later on something about, I'm sure, a most important accessory, the rear sere retainer keeper pin and spring. I was amazed that guns ever worked, especially as they were prone to various stoppages. What one was supposed to do if such an occasion arose, I hated to think, as most guns in aeroplanes were in their wings or within the fuselage and way out of reach of the pilot.

CHAPTER SEVEN
Rigging and engine runs

Having made sure the Continental ninety horsepower engine on the front of the S.E.5a was going to stay there, the next thing was to take it out again. This Des and I managed to do with only a little swearing and chewing of fingers, which got caught in the winch strings. The undercarriage was removed, so also the tail plane. We were back to lots of bits in no time, but for a good reason. The whole lot had to be moved to larger premises for the fitting of the wings and the rigging of the same.

The site chosen was a disused church hall, at one time used as a temporary church and still bearing the raised platform at one end where the altar would have been and with windows shedding ecclesiastical beams of light through the quadriform glass. I thought, on first entry, that the odour of sanctity still prevailed, but on further investigation found it to be a mixture of mildew and bird droppings. The place had long since suffered from the 'change of use' and no longer could claim connections with the diocese.

The disused church hall

Fortunately, this place was owned by a good friend of mine and was not too far from home. A helpful member of the local LAA Strut loaned me his ancient trailer and by the second journey all the bits were spread around the hall. The fuselage transported very well; only the undercarriage, which was a separate item, and was roped onto the rear of the trailer tried to escape. The wings, being wings, attempted to fly. Nicely slotted into their cradle and padded with cushions, I thought they were secure. Not so. At thirty miles an hour the cushions took off first and were scattered in the road behind. The wings were trying hard to follow, till a reassessment and extra rope put paid to their ideas. A good omen really.

I had, in spare moments, constructed some trestles, each about eight feet tall, with two cross pieces which could be adjusted for the height of the wings when they were attached to the fuselage. By juggling the height and slope of these cross pieces, I could bring the wings to approximately their dihedral and incidence angles. All the wings, fuselage, tail plane, undercarriage, trestles, bits and pieces, tools, wires and what-have-you were crammed into the ex-church hall.

When I had first viewed the premises as an empty shell, it looked big enough to build Concorde. Now I realised that, although the length could easily take the wing span, the width was only just big enough for the fuselage with tail attached and even that meant hoisting the fuselage into the flying position with the tail above the ancient tortoise stove.

Many hands certainly made light work. Hefties seemed to appear from nowhere as soon as we arrived with the last pieces. The fuselage was carried ceremoniously into the nave, and with enough willing strong men, held while I slipped the bolts into position to hold the undercarriage in place. Now on its wheels, the fuselage could be trundled to the middle of the hall and set across its width.

Before we left for home that evening, the whole plane was covered with protective sheets. I could see the resident starlings watching proceedings from cracks and niches in the structure of the building and waiting to secure their new perches with small deposits.

It was early spring when the rigging began and I was plagued, the whole time, by these residents being a confounded nuisance with their constant nesting, chatter and mess. Maybe they had a greater claim to being there than I had; after all, they had been there for generations. I had hoped that they, as flying creatures, would respect another flying machine. Whether what they put on was their stamp of approval or disapproval, I was never sure.

After screwing together and erecting the trestles and arranging the cross-pieces at the approximate height, Liz and I heaved the top wings into place, she inching the wing over the hurdle-like trestle from half-way up a rickety wooden pair of steps, while I, from a position on yet another swaying platform, tried desperately to align the wing brackets into the matching ones of the centre section. Using four inch nails, instead of the five-sixteenths of an inch bolts, made things a little simpler for the initial wing-hanging. The real bolts could wait until all the wings were more or less in place and balancing the weight on each side of the fuselage.

I had done a little trying out of wing attaching when still at home, with the top wings spread across the garden, resting on tables with the centre section positioned slightly lower to create the dihedral. It had, more or less, worked, then after measuring from wing tip to a point a few feet in front of the centre of the centre section, I had discovered no great discrepancy.

By the time both top wings were hung on, I was struck, really for the first time, that all these bits when put together, were going to look like an aeroplane. Up to now all the separate pieces spread around the various sheds at home, and even when spread around the church hall, looked only like a collection of aircraft components. Now, as the bottom wings were threaded through the lower cross-pieces of the trestles and pinned onto the fuselage brackets, the true size and shape began to emerge.

The realisation that it was going to work and it was going to be a real aeroplane and that I could well be flying it in about six months' time came as an exhilarating shock. I couldn't wait to get it finished.

Where flying is concerned I have this almost uncontrollable urge to 'get to it'. I have always found myself driving faster and faster as I approach any particular airfield where there is some flying in the offing. I had, somehow, to submerge this urge, put the brakes on, slow down, take it easy and be sure to work painstakingly with great control and care, or I'd be sure to start making mistakes.

My next move was to put in position the inter-plane struts, or at least the temporary ones that I had made from rough old wood, to see if any adjustments were needed in their length. When positioned, they held the wings apart, so that when the bottom wing was lifted to give the three degree dihedral, the top wing would follow suit. By tilting the cross members of the trestle, the wing should rest flat upon it at more or less the right incidence angle. These angles would be eventually controlled by the bracing wires stretched diagonally between various struts. Before any wires were positioned, a certain amount of checking was necessary, using various gauges, which I had made, and a clinometer which I had borrowed. I had ordered the bracing wire months before from a firm in Canada which, unknown to me, had ceased trading even before my order had reached them. It was some time before anyone wrote to say so.

I put this down to the usual wait one came to expect from most firms who purport to sell aircraft materials. Just a few are prompt, civil, helpful and generally on the side of the customer. I always pass their names onto likely buyers. It was such a firm, somewhere near Norwich, who found the wire I was looking for. Made up of nineteen strands of tough stainless steel, this wire was given a breaking strain of twenty-one hundred pounds. On test it was even better.

Thirty-four turnbuckles were used to stress the rigging of the wings, tailplane and undercarriage, the wire being held on to them by it passing around a thimble and into a Nicopress sleeve. The original way of forming the eye was to wire splice around the thimble. I would like to have used that method, but I knew my fingers would never do it and, from what I have heard since, one's eyesight gives up in the process. The sleeves, when properly squeezed by the special tool, were tested. The wire broke before they did.

S.E.5a assembled in the church hall

Before the actual wire bracing process began, I had to fix up a bench with a sizeable vice to hold the Nicopress tool, an iron plate and cold chisel to neatly cut the wire, and then, most important, a sit down with a cup of tea to give me time to think out the best procedure.

There were to be six flying wires, four landing wires, four incidence wires, eight centre section wires, which I had fitted before leaving home, four undercarriage wires and eight tail plane wires. I started with the undercarriage bracing in the knowledge that, if I made a mess of them, at least they were short enough to make again without wasting too much material. All went well. I was surprised how solid everything felt when the turnbuckles were tweaked up. On to the rest with much more confidence and I think, by and large, I made no major mistakes.

It was a great help to have Liz there as a steadying influence to stop my mad rush into trouble and to hold the other end of the wire. After attaching the landing wires, two each side, I, in a fit of bravado, swung away the trestles. Nothing collapsed. The wings just stayed there, comfortably supported and looking at ease. After this, it was just a question of getting down to hard graft, repeating the process of eye clamping, measuring and turnbuckling. The hardest part was to come; tuning the wires to obtain a constant incidence angle along each wing and the same both sides. It all came right eventually and still maintained the right dihedral. The birdcage of wires produced an immensely strong structure. The tail plane presented no problems and stood with its wings horizontal and the fin vertical and all nicely rigid.

Friends and strangers looked in to see progress and encourage the workers. Bill Goldfinch, of Colditz Castle glider fame, came to give his blessing and try the cockpit for size. I promised him a flight when the S.E.5a was airworthy, as I had flown his Luton Minor after he had completed it some years before.

Yet again, some sceptics stood eyeing the plane as if calculating the strength of every component and slowly shaking their heads whilst drawing in a very deep breath. I always expected some wisdom pearl to fall but, as like as not, all that happened was a pitying look, a slow heel turn and exit left. I was too busy to argue with them as one of my last jobs to do before dismantling everything was to attach labels to every wire noting their position, left or right and for what purpose they were to be used.

By mid-March all was completed on the rigging side, so the return journeys were got under way. It had been a cold business working within the ecclesiastical corrugated iron. I was glad to get back to my own shed with its three kilowatt fan heater making life bearable. This time the engine was going in for good. The engine mounting bolts, which had been on order for at least a year, had arrived. The engine mounts were collected from a firm only eighty miles away. The scaffold tower was, once again, brought into use, the hoist made ready for hoisting. As a challenge I dragged the engine, kicking and screaming, into place single-handed. Halfway through I wished I hadn't, but after rude and encouraging words from me, it gave up and the bolts were slipped home. More tea after that. Time for the fingers to recover.

The instructions in the plans said 'Make suitable cowlings', then gave some basic ideas as to how it could be done. My idea of suitable cowlings necessitated them to be easily removable, apart from looking something like the lines of the original S.E.5a. I drew out a few possibilities without too much detail, but in the end concluded I'd make it up as I went along, loosely following my drawings. First and foremost was the radiator front. False, of course, as my engine is air-cooled. I decided to make a copy of the radiator used by the later marks of S.E., of about 1918.

Copy was a bit ambitious. What I ended up with was a rather inaccurate impression of the real thing. Once again, I suppose, it was the best I could do with my limited skill and very limited workshop facilities. Since seeing what wonders some other people have done in the business of copying S.E.5a radiators, I can only say, "I did my best." I do know that mine took a long time to design and longer to make.

When it was eventually placed onto the front of the aeroplane, I could easily see where the next pieces of the cowling would have to go. The whole cowling had to box in the engine, without actually touching it, otherwise, as the engine vibrated on its rubber mountings, they would be rattled to pieces. I made the side panels easily detachable by using Dzus fasteners, which quickly and easily twist and lock panels in place to enable inspection to all parts. The false rocker box covers hinged up and over, allowing plugs to be easily inspected or changed. Inside the cowling, the blast of air from the front was directed by baffles around and between the cylinders to give adequate cooling. At least that was the theory. I'm still experimenting with air flow patterns. I'm sure, by looking at the temperature gauge, that the engine is being cooled sufficiently, but this is winter. What will happen in hot weather, if any, I shall find out later. The exhaust leaves the cylinders through short stub-pipes branching into long tubes which reach right back to the cockpit as per original S.E. I have taken my exhausts just a little way further back so that the blasting diapason is slightly behind my ears, instead of right alongside as the old ones were.

It does mean I can hear the noise of the aeolian bracing wires and it has even been known for me to distinguish some of what the chaps have said on the radio. I should say I'm against using radio.

I only use it if I have to. So far, I'm experimenting with it. I have always considered radio to be a link with the ground and with my present kind of flying that's just what I can do without.

Surrounding the first eighteen inches of exhaust pipe are, on both sides of the engine, heat exchangers, collecting cold air from the front, warming it up a bit, and passing it, on one side, to the carburettor and on the other side to the bottom of the cockpit where my feet are. Carburettor 'hot air' is controlled, on or off, by a cable from the cockpit to be selected when required. It can be very necessary if icing conditions are experienced. Engines and ice do not go well together. The cockpit heater, although not great, at least keeps me from freezing.

All this cowling, designing, making, fitting, re-fitting, and general juggling coupled with the connecting of all the engine controls took weeks instead of days. I should have known by now that everything to do with aircraft building takes longer than imagined. The first engine run did not take place until mid-summer. Again, a certain amount of waiting was encountered, this time for new ignition leads. I suppose I could have used the old ones, but they looked as if they had been around as long as I have. So, sparing no expense, I ordered new ones and waited.

The engine run was to be conducted in my back garden. First, a warning to the neighbours. They were awfully decent, even taking enough interest to peer over the hedges to watch proceedings. Second, remove half the front of the workshop to ease the fuselage out onto the back lawn, tie the tail down and put chocks in place. Third, make sure enough petrol was in the tank and reaching the carburettor. Then the moment of truth.

Des elected to swing the propeller. The resigned look on his face indicated that, after four years sitting doing nothing, the engine was not likely to start readily. From my perch in the cockpit, I felt like a vicar who had climbed to the pulpit to give his sermon and realised he'd forgotten his text. It all came back by the time I'd looked around and placed my hands on the throttle and switches. Petrol on, throttle closed, switches off, suck in. Des turned the prop. I primed with the pump. Throttle set, contact. I switched the ignition on and Des swung the prop.

First engine run at home

No, it didn't start first swing, but it did on the second. Away it went, one thousand revs per minute. The noise in the confined space of the garden was horrendous. Next door's cat, who up till then had been watching from the hedge bottom, vanished and was not seen for the next two days. The neighbours retreated, some sure it would fly to pieces, some sure that it might fly prematurely, even though the wings were not affixed. After checking oil pressure and temperature, throttle control, slow running and ignition switches, I closed it all down, feeling very pleased with it and myself. The neighbours said, "Will you be doing that again?" I felt I'd better not. I said I was sorry for all the inconvenience I had caused.

CHAPTER EIGHT
Little Rissington, Charterhall and Blenheims

The late summer of 1942 in the Cotswolds was serene. Little Rissington, the aerodrome perched on the hill above Bourton-on-the-Water in Gloucestershire, was home for the next few weeks. All of us pilots who had survived the courses so far were there, waiting for postings to Operational Training Units. We even managed to arrange a week's leave, and it was during my journey to Southampton, when I had to change trains at Eastleigh, that I bumped into Cliff, my old school friend, whom I hadn't seen since Uxbridge days. He was also going on leave, but for a rather different reason. He had been a rear gunner for ages, flying out over the Bay of Biscay patrolling in an ancient Whitley bomber. Somehow or other it had caught fire. Staggering back to Cornwall, the poor thing just made land when the pilot realised it would fall apart, so gave the order to bail out. All the crew were very eager to leave and did so, all that is, except the pilot, who probably hung on too long and died with his crippled aeroplane.

Cliff told me all this on the short train journey into Southampton West station. We then went our separate ways home. I have never seen him since. He survived the war and, I believe, stayed on in the RAF for a while before going into business.

Back at Rissington, flying Oxfords to fill in time was a great way to learn the English countryside from the air. The maps we were issued with were very limited, covering only our local area. The only way to overcome this was to go and find out. Striking off westward at a fairly low altitude, I found myself suddenly surmounting a rise and then plummeting over a most amazing stone city, built into the contours of the hillsides - a most glorious sight. Checking my school-boy atlas which I carried for reference, I realised I was over the magnificent city of Bath.

Again, knowing that my brother had been moved to a shadow factory in Hungerford, the Southampton factory having been badly bombed, I flew south. His factory was very easy to find. It was the only camouflaged building in the whole of Hungerford and stuck out like a sore thumb.

Yet another trip took me to the South, this time to Embley Park, the home of Florence Nightingale, which is close to Romsey and just north of Southampton. My father's office had been evacuated there from the docks after most of it had been blown to bits. Embley was easy to find, as the balloon barrage at Southampton could be seen for miles. The grand house, set in its park, stood out well, and as I flew low up the lawn, I could see my father waving from his high office window. Later, when I called there, on foot, I was admonished by an ancient retainer who was worried about losing his chimneys.

For a whole month a number of us were taken by bus every evening, some miles from Rissington to a small airfield near Minster Lovell in Oxfordshire, called Akeman Street, to practise night flying. It was called Akeman Street because the Roman Road of that name passed through its outer edge. Our circuit took us over the town of Witney. Circuits and bumps again by the dozen, but at night and, what a change from Rhodesia, in the blackout. I began to realise that I enjoyed night flying, possibly more than flying in daylight. I was not sure why - possibly because of the mystery, possibly because you can't see the danger.

Gradually the course members were posted away, some to bomber O.T.U.s quite close to Little Rissington, some miles away in Yorkshire and Lincolnshire. The big four-engined bombers were making a name for themselves, but the O.T.U.s were still using mainly Wellingtons. I was not looking forward to driving those lumbering aeroplanes.

Eventually, my posting came through - posted to 51 O.T.U. Charter Hall. Frantic enquiries and searchings told me that this place was somewhere near Berwick-upon-Tweed, where they trained for night fighters. The dog with two tails wasn't in it. Fighters at last and now at night – wonderful!

Two of us actually went from Rissy, a quiet New Zealander, and me. He had about as much idea of where Berwick-upon-Tweed was as I had - it was the blind leading the blind. First to London, across on the tube to Kings Cross, then northwards through the night, arriving at six in the morning. Train travel in war-time was not to be recommended. On this trip we portered our own three kit-bags and two cases each, which was fun on the underground, and then had to stand the whole journey from start to finish. Stand meant standing in the corridor guarding all the equipment while half the British Army, wearing tin hats on one shoulder and a rifle on the other and their kitbags slung across both, pushed past. Chugging by local puffer brought us to Greenlaw, the nearest station to Charter Hall.

The last mile or so we managed in the ration wagon, which had met the train for what appeared to be a few tons of vegetables with which we were to ride. After we had been there a while, we found that the nearest towns were Kelso, about seven miles to the South, and Coldstream about six miles South-East. The nearest large town was Berwick-upon-Tweed, some fifteen miles to the East. The 'drome had hard runways, the first I'd really come across, and was miles away from the dispersed living quarters. These quarters were Nissen huts, semi-cylindrical huts made from corrugated iron. They were made in various sizes, little ones for bedrooms and an enormous one for the mess and recreation rooms.

The whole site was windswept, desolate and extremely cold. My own hut had a small tortoise-stove at one end of the room which, if fed correctly and with the wind in the right direction, could be coaxed to become red-hot. It was still not sufficient to melt the ice-puddle which formed when rain and snow blew in from the other end. I slept in more clothes than I wore during the day. My Irvin suit, a vast affair of sheepskin leather jacket and trousers, furry side inside, formed my sleeping bag. There were no baths, only showers and these had the usual great gap top and bottom, and no doors. I braved a shower on very few occasions. I expect we all smelled pretty horrible after a while.

Slaughterhall was the local name for this station and after visiting it lately, I found that it is still called that name by the older natives. It lived up to its name during my stay. Buses plied to and from the camp and the flights. Based on normal bus services, they left just before you got to the stop, then the gap between the next one was just a little longer than it took to walk the mile and a half.

Half way through the course I had a bicycle sent from home, which gave me some independence.

I was there with the intention of becoming a night-fighter pilot, and the course would cover instruction on three types of Bristol Blenheim aeroplanes, eventually leading to flying the Beaufighter, which was the standard night-fighter aircraft. Also during the course I would be teamed with a Radar Operator to control the magic box, known as the Mark 4 AI (for Airborne Interception).

Scotland, between the months of November and February, has real winter weather, especially around Charterhall which was built in a saucer-like depression in the landscape.

Bristol Blenheim Mk IV

The aeroplanes used for initial training were the Blenheims 1, 1V, and V's, all very much the same in some respects, but very different in others. The outwardly visible bits had similarities - all the same wings, tails, undercarriages and fuselages from the wings back, and all used the same Bristol Mercury engines, although of different marks. The differences were in the front styling, the flying characteristics, the position of various gadgets and the pilot's visibility. The Mk.1 was a sprightly craft, the Mk. 1V more lumbering and with the nose built out so that a bomb aimer could get into the front to operate his bomb-sight, but that meant the pilot could hardly see anything to the right of the built-up glasshouse.

The Blenheim V on which my initial instruction began, was a much larger aircraft than I had flown before and was heavier than all the others. The wingspan seemed to stretch outwards for miles past the engines, of which there was one each side of the dual-control cockpit. The long, glass-covered nose pushed out in front, sloping to a point and giving me a reasonable view. I soon found out why the instructor preferred the Mark V, it had a heated cockpit, unlike the Blenheims I and IV which were draughty ice-boxes.

Getting into the cockpit was achieved by climbing up over the wing from the rear, a climb which almost needed an alpenstock. Dropping in from above for the first time, I found myself sitting next to my instructor; my namesake, F/O Gregory. When seated, it became obvious that ergonomics were not a great consideration when designing the cockpit. Taps, levers, gauges and more levers were scattered around willy-nilly. Throttles and pitch controls were easily grasped, so that during take-off the left hand controlled the power. Raising the undercarriage needed a quick change of hands to pull up the undercarriage lever, which was close to the right-hand side of the pilot's seat. The standard blind-flying panel was where it should be, facing the pilot, but engine instruments, rev counters and temperature and pressure gauges all had to be looked for.

F/O Gregory was full of joy and a pleasure to fly with. He expected me to find difficulties and make mistakes, then he would quietly explain again, until I got things right. I found taxiing particularly difficult. The lag between the engine throttle opening and the aircraft turning was quite marked, so that by the time I got round to anticipating the swing the other way and had used opposite throttle to correct, we were going faster and faster along the perimeter track. The electrically-operated cowling gills were a blessing compared with the manual ones on the other marks. Closing cowling gills for take-off was essential to getting off the ground; if they were not closed, you were not getting airborne.

Then, watching the temperatures rise and opening them again before things got too hot. Great lumps of built-in drag were incorporated into this rather old design of aeroplane, all trying to stop it rising from the earth.

The propellers could be set into fine pitch or coarse. Fine was for take-off where maximum revolutions were necessary, and on the final approach for landing, in case an overshoot was undertaken. Coarse pitch was for cruise, where economy played a part and for higher speeds. Keeping straight became easier as the tail came off the ground. The undercarriage was raised by pulling up a handle, very reminiscent of the galvanised handle on the end of an old-fashioned lavatory chain, situated alongside the right-hand edge of my seat. It was one of three handles so you had to be sure which was which. This one was covered with a flap across the top to prevent accidental use, which removed pieces of knuckle every time.

It was then necessary to change into coarse pitch by groping behind the seat to pull out two mushroom-shaped knobs. Then, on the Blenheim I and IV, to wind open the cowling gills enough to stop overheating yet still without restricting the climb too much. With both hands searching for knobs and levers, it was easy to forget that the aircraft still had to be flown and at night it could be quite a problem. All marks of Blenheim suffered with these strange arrangements of controls, whose positions were learned slowly and painfully.

Painful, too, were the cutting draughts which stabbed through the ill-fitting panels. These pitiable old things had taken a battering from years of riggers removing and replacing inspection panels, covers and hatches. Bits, I'm sure, had fallen off, leaving small holes for the well-below-zero Scottish winds to scream through. After an hour or so, I found myself frozen, with arms and legs absolutely solid. The cold penetrated all clothing consisting, in my case, of first from the inside; me, still in my pyjamas, then two pairs of long johns and vests, shirt, large white pullover, uniform battle dress, Irvin suit, flying boots and socks, scarves, two pairs of gloves and the flying helmet and oxygen mask. The only uncovered parts were a pair of eyes surveying the bleakness.

We were told that the use of oxygen, would, to a certain extent, keep one warm. On an oxygen climb to twenty thousand feet, one of the exercises we had to do, I found little benefit. Actually, had there been any benefit, I would have missed out as the tube connector was not working and I did the climb not realising that there was no oxygen supply.

Taking all things into consideration though, the Blenheim V was a pleasant aircraft to fly and after three trips with my instructor I was sent off solo in a Blenheim I. This was known as the short-nosed Blenheim, nice enough, but in the Scottish winter, very cold.

After three solo trips in the Blenheim I, I was sent off in a Blenheim IV.

The winter of 1942 in Scotland became very white very early on. Skimming low over the snow-covered Cheviot Hills was a real treat. They were big enough and rounded enough for a Blenheim to follow the contours without a great variation of control. Charterhall, being in a slight hollow, had its own weather conditions, generally worse than the surrounding countryside, so that a slight change from the usual east wind would raise the temperature just enough to produce thick fog. This particular day started well with clear sky and slight mist, just right for the exercise I had to carry out. After an hour I returned to Charterhall to be told that it was closed due to thick fog and that I was to be vectored around the area by the ground controller, who would be giving me courses to steer, until either the fog cleared or another aerodrome was found which could accept us.

Although I was wearing fur-lined trousers and jacket, the cold crept into me as I sat there like a stone statue. A wintry sun was shining where I was, well up above the layer of fog. My whole world was like being in a hazy goldfish bowl, only the occasional words from the ground kept me in touch with reality, but even that was of little comfort. After three hours of purgatory I could see my petrol gauges were well down and I was not quite sure how much longer the engines would keep on turning.

As a very junior and miserable sergeant pilot, I felt it was not my place to complain too loudly, but by the next message from the ground I did point out the situation, only to be told they were aware of the problem and would do their best to solve it. More sitting in the cold and worrying, until in desperation I called the ground and really expressed my anxiety as the gauges were reading nearly empty. "Steer North and reduce height to 1,000 feet," was the reply. At first I wondered if I was to be told to bale out, which I would have to do if the engines stopped, but then came the encouraging message "We think Drem may be clearing and will direct you there." Drem was a reasonably small grass airfield which had been camouflaged by the marking out in creosote of fake square fields so that the boundaries were difficult to see. At 500 feet I could just make out green countryside when the scattered fog allowed glimpses of the ground. The directions I had been given must either have been very good or very lucky, because within a short time of my circling around, I spied a green Very light (a pyrotechnic) being shot up at me. Somehow I judged the extent of the field and got down safely, but had to stay at Drem overnight until Charterhall cleared.

The Chief Flying Instructor seemed so pleased to get both his student and his aircraft back that he wrote a commendation in my log-book. Little did he know what was going to happen in ten nights time. Just a few days before Christmas 1942, Charterhall was in a most belligerent mood and I was sent on my first night flying exercise in a Blenheim I. The take-off was into the blackness, flying on instruments until the horizon could be defined with stars appearing to reach all the way to the ground. At ten thousand feet my world was a cold and lonely place, my only comfort was the glowing red exhaust rings at the front of the engines.

Ground control kept me flying course after course with no information as to what was happening elsewhere. Again, hours passed without being recalled to land at Charterhall. It took me very little time to realise that once again fog had collected in the saucer-shaped territory around Charterhall. I was not the only one in the air, I could hear other worried pilots calling base and asking for diversions. Again petrol was getting low but all my warnings to those on the ground were to no avail.

By now, several others in the air were shouting for help and declaring that they MUST be brought down, and eventually I called saying that my petrol gauges were reading zero, which they were. I was worried that should one or both engines stop I would have to bale out, and I worried whether I was over land or the Firth of Forth, which I knew could not be far away. In the darkness of the cockpit I tried to figure out how to open the door in the nose of the aircraft, Clambering out through the top hatch was out of the question, because as soon as you were in the slipstream the chances were that you would slide down the fuselage and hit the tailplane.

As I could see no way out through the front, I decided to stay and hope that my earnest prayers would be answered and somewhere could be found where the fog was thin enough for me to land. Again I appealed to those below, explaining again that the petrol gauges were reading empty. At last I got an order to fly a new course and descend from ten thousand feet to one thousand. I flew as accurately as I possibly could, using the instruments because what faint horizon I had previously seen had disappeared.

Flying over fog it is possible, if the fog is not too thick, to see bright lights directly below because you are only looking through a comparatively thin layer, whereas looking obliquely through that layer it would be impenetrable. Soon I glimpsed a row of runway lights and was then surrounded by pyrotechnics being fired up into the foggy atmosphere. Mortars, rockets and even Very cartridges lit the sky.

I pushed the nose into a dive towards the firework display and found myself about three hundred feet above the runway, although my altimeter was reading two hundred feet below ground. In seconds I had overflown the runway, but at least I knew its direction. Remembering the method I had been taught of flying blind approaches, I steered thirty degrees right by my compass, counted off a minute, carried out a rate one turn to the left on to the reciprocal heading from the runway I had just passed over, and the lights appeared again. I was a few feet too high and slightly off course, but after banging down the undercarriage and flaps I touched down with one wheel on the hard runway and one on the frozen earth beside it. I had enough speed to drag the thing onto the hard stuff, but had to swivel round at the end to stop myself becoming bogged down. I must have used nearly all the runway's length, but still managed to stop and turn off the tarmac, then report that I was down and clear. I had never been more pleased to be in the arms of Mother Earth having been airborne for four hours.

I had been frightened. I was even more frightened the next day. Looking out over the countryside the morning after, I was shattered to see the terrain over which I had flown that very low circuit. It was dotted with hillocks, between which I must have flown, missing them by not too much. Thinking back over the years, I know there were many things I should have done and possibly a few things I should not have done. East Fortune was my diversion airfield, an aerodrome famous for airships in the early days and now a museum.

I had been very lucky, but not everyone was. Poor unfortunate Richard Hillary, the author of the best-selling war book, *The Last Enemy*, was one of my course members who was killed. We all admired him greatly. His press-on attitude, after having suffered so much from his burning crash during the Battle of Britain, showed more than great determination. His face and hands had been remade at East Grinstead by the miracle workers in skin grafting, though he still presented a picture of suffering. My own opinion at the time was, and still is, that however much he badgered people of high rank to let him return to flying, he should never have been allowed to fly at night. He was essentially a day fighter pilot. He was a great loss.

Just before Christmas we pilots were to be crewed with our navigators. A tricky business, we were told. We were also told to make sure our chosen crew member was compatible with our own personality, as clashes could be hopeless, and if anyone was not sure about his navigator, he could change him for another. I expect the navigators were told something the same about pilots. I have called them 'navigators', which is what they were eventually called. At that time all wore a single-winged badge with the initials 'R.O.' worked on them. This was to be read as Radio

Operator or Radar Operator, depending on who was referring to them. Some considered the very word 'radar' as so secret as only to be spoken of in hushed tones. Night fighting was becoming a science, where the stalking of the enemy was carried out without setting human eyes on the target until the last moment, and at very close range. All else was done by directions, either from controllers on the ground, or from your own radar in the aircraft, operated by these boffins called R.O.s.

These R.O.s were specialists. They collected in small groups and talked secretly about cathode ray tubes and blips and traces and ground returns and other unintelligible gadgetry. Some R.O.s wore spectacles, not often seen in aircrew. Some, I'm sure, carried soldering irons and fuses permanently in their pockets. Some were old, even as old as thirty. Eagerly I scanned the lists and found I was to be teamed with one D.H. Stephens. Pilots and R.O.s were milling around like an all-male Paul Jones, and asking, "Do you know what's-his-name?''

Someone pointed out this man Stephens to me. By then, this tall, dark-haired and hawk-like featured man was advancing on me. We introduced ourselves with a rather self-conscious handshake, eyeing each other suspiciously. I think at the back of both of our minds was the thought, 'Will we get on with each other or shall we swap for someone different?'

Doug and 'Steve', firm friends

By the time the evening had worn on and the ice was broken over a drink or two, we were both convinced that we would have no troubles flying together.

We were firm friends from that day on and still flew together at least once a year when the opportunity arose until his death. It was at the beginning of my S.E.5a project that Steve presented me with a band-saw that he felt was surplus to his requirement - a great asset. Then later he bought me a radio to be used in the aircraft.

CHAPTER NINE
Final assembly of the dream

August Bank Holiday Monday was S.E.5a moving day. I couldn't bear the thought of repeating the open trailer move of last time. Forty miles was a long way to expect it to 'stay put' on what amounted to a vehicular flight-deck. A local home removal service came to the rescue with an enormous furniture van. All I had to do was to take the centre section off the fuselage, dismantle one side of my shed, wheel the fuselage out, replace and re-rig the centre section, add on things like guns and exhaust pipes, then wheel it all round, squeezing past the side of the house to the front garden. The wings and tail were trolleyed back home from a garage up the road, where they had been stored. The trestles, steps and stands were assembled in my garage. All was ready for the great day.

Loading into the removal firm's truck

The van arrived at nine o'clock on the quiet Monday morning. Three giants accompanied it. I should have said gentle giants. The loving care taken to load everything on board astonished me. Everything was carefully loaded with ample cushioning. Chunks of foam were stuffed into every corner. Blankets covered all the wings, protecting them from anything which might have damaged them. I was extremely pleased with the efficiency of those removers. They told me that moving aeroplanes was not in their usual line of business. I think they quite enjoyed the new experience.

After two hours they were ready to move off. I hurried on to Boscombe Down to inform the security police that the move was under way. I had told them some days before, so they were not altogether surprised when the vast van turned up at their locked gate. By the time the van and I had reached our hangar, it was time for late coffee.

Assembled at Boscombe Down

Unloading took a fraction of the loading time and soon all the bits, wings, fuselage and gear was sitting around inside the hangar. Away went the van, while we had lunch and considered the best way to start the assembly. Up with the trestles, out with the steps, up and over with the wings and push the bolts in. It looked like an aeroplane by the end of the afternoon.

Word travels fast, so that by the next morning, after I'd only been there a few minutes, small groups of admirers arrived to look. Although they stopped me working, I was extremely pleased to think they showed an interest, and in the case of these people who knew about aeroplanes, an intelligent interest. Many, many people, from the Group Captain down to the lowly apprentice, called to give their blessing.

Even though I had rigged the S.E. in the church hall, it still took over two weeks to put it together again. Gradually, it took on a more business-like look. Wings were attached properly, turnbuckles tightened and wire locked. The control rods were connected so that full movement was achieved on the elevators and the differential ailerons did what they should do. I fitted stops on the rudder, as its movement was great enough to foul the elevators. The fillets joining the centre section to the top wings were pasted on, so also the gap strips between the bottom wing and fuselage. On and on, there seemed no end to all the little bits which had to be done. I made list after list of the jobs to be finished. I nearly forgot to join up the airspeed indicator to the pitot tube. I must have used dozens of split pins to lock all the clevis studs. My inspector, an ex-Boscombe Down king-pin, kept a watchful eye on the proceedings. Nothing ever escapes his eagle eye. He can spot where a split pin is missing or a locking wire wrongly wound from at least a hundred yards.

The fuel flow test took little time and was O.K. The visitors and watchers started to enquire, "When's the great day?" I knew it was getting close and in my eagerness tried to hurry things along, but was restrained by Liz, who kept on about, "No short cuts, now that you have got this far."

A good long engine run, long enough to get the oil hot, brought to light one or two oil leaks. The one quite bad one from a deformed rocker box cover, necessitated removing the thing, hitting it with a hammer until it submitted then, with an extra gasket, refitting and hoping. Two or three applications of the big hammer were needed before the oil stopped seeping.

The LAA requirement, before first flight, was to have all stages of the building, inspected and signed for. This was done during the stages of building and sent to be filed to the LAA office. Now that the project was reaching its conclusion, a lot more information was required. Careful weighing of the aircraft had to take place so that the centre of gravity could be worked out and shown to be within the limits of the design. Des, being much more of a mathematician than I shall ever be, took it upon himself, I am pleased to say, to work out all figures. We were within limits. After more form filling, stating such things as serial numbers of instruments, engine data, propeller data and log books, the whole lot was parcelled up and sent to the LAA office. Included was my request for me to test my own aircraft. This was granted after I had disclosed my past flying experience. All the necessary bumph was returned in record time and all approved. The permission to test was enclosed.

All the time while I had been working in the hangar to bring the S.E. up to flying state, the weather outside had held on to a high pressure system, creating calm, misty conditions, the haziness lasting all day, keeping the visibility down to a couple of miles. I was hoping against hope that nothing would change these conditions, they were just right for a first flight. I couldn't believe that these ideal flying days could possibly last. I could stand the tension no longer. I made a desperate effort to bring everything to readiness. Des was told it was 'on' and arrived at four o'clock on Wednesday, 16th September. Liz had been working with me all day, and my son came along after he had finished work to see the fun, if any, and to help with the pushing. I alerted the fire brigade, telling them it was to be the first flight. The friendly station police got to know and promised attendance. Apart from Des and me and our respective wives, my son, two other club members who by chance happened to be there, and the very large six-wheeled fire engine and crew, plus the police Land Rover, no-one was there to spectate.

As military flying finished and the 'drome officially closed, we pushed the S.E. the mile-long trek to the grass strip which we hoped would be more or less into wind. There was very little wind, but what was blowing was slightly across the length of the strip. I tried hard to look as casual as possible as I donned my

Irvin Jacket, helmet and gloves. It all felt like my first flying day way back in Rhodesia when the apprehension and anticipation made everything go a bit blurred. Beneath the surface I was excited. More excited than was good for an old chap of my age. A touch of the dry mouth solo-itis crept in. Des helped me to strap in, I primed the engine and went through the starting drill. Des swung the prop. It started. I was determined to give the engine ample time to warm up. The plan was to warm up the engine until the oil temperature started to read on the gauge, taxi out to mid-grass, then do a number of fast runs to get the feel of the aeroplane. It seemed to take ages to get the engine to a reasonable temperature. I just sat there.

CHAPTER TEN
Beaufighters to Germany

Beaufighter evening

East Anglia looked purple in the late evening light
The summer sunset slowly crept away
We crawled climbing to our height
As haze foretold the quiet fading day

Steve set the course for me to try to keep
My mind was faintly musing, as in a dream
The throbbing engines sent me half asleep
My thoughts became a muzzy swirling stream

I could just view the roads, near traffic free
With cottages and hamlets fading in the gloom
And little ponds and rills, shining back at me
Reflecting the brightness of the early rising moon

I could just make out, or imagined, I could see
Little people off to enjoy their evening out
Then I recalled when we'd last had an evening free
And wondered quite what our life was all about

So there we were stuck way up in the air
Wishing we were down there with our crowd
I muttered to myself, "It isn't really fair
This kind of thing should never be allowed."

T'was then my mind flashed back to days gone by
With all the good times we'd had up to date
We'd done damned well, and that we can't deny
And we hoped to have plenty more as great

Then looking down I clearly saw old Norwich town
And remembered going to Victoria Hospital dance
When all those gorgeous nurses trotted down
All those lovelies, well worth a second glance

I spent a lot of time in the Bull's long bar
My; we had some fun, and sang some awful songs
I think we may have gone a bit too far
Perhaps we should have known the rights from wrongs

Gawd; that night in Fakenham's town hall
Where we danced and boozed the night away
We didn't get back home to bed at all
Then staggered into the mess around midday

What was the name of that gorgeous peach
I met at a hop in the Dukes Head, Kings Lynn
A bit snooty, posh and a little out of reach
She could even have caused a holy saint to sin

She was a Wren, a right smasher, and cute
Her blouse was just a little bit too tight
I'd never seen anything in a sailor suit
That looked so uniformly right

Then I thought what my poor old mum would have said
If she had known how low her dear son could sink
I reckon she would have quickly passed away
Or have six fits, then taken to strong drink

Steve woke me with a derisive shout
As he'd been plotting courses from the Gee
Yelled for God's sake, get your finger out
You're wandering about, can't you see

Look ahead and find the line of coastal strand
It should be Walcheren just about ahead
See all that flak over on our right hand
Just ease it over slightly to the left instead.

By now I was concentrating, wide awake
And Steve was back, head stuffed in his set
Said, "Get her climbing up a bit, for goodness sake."
I'm still jammed with ground returns, as yet.

The night was long and cold with chases few
I was so glad when the cruel North Sea passed once more
At least we'd tried, what we'd been sent out to do
No heroic darings, no Huns to boost our score

We got back home unscathed and quite alright
It was jolly good to see yet another day
And so to bed, although it was nearly light
Steve said, "Down the pub again tonight, O.K."

Back at Slaughterhall, Steve and I were getting used to the radar interception exercises in our Blenheims, which we performed during the day and at night. The Scottish Christmas had come and gone, almost unnoticed by the natives, who I'm sure were not then converted to Christianity; I'm not sure whether they are yet. Snow covered almost everything, except when the wind changed and it rained. Whatever the weather did or did not do, it remained extremely cold. We again fell foul of authority when we both, forcing our way through a blizzard, failed to see and salute the adjutant. This pompous groundling ordered Steve to spend the whole afternoon standing outside his office, saluting any officer who might pass. Why I got away with it I'm not sure. It must have made Steve a much better radar operator. I sometimes wondered who the real enemy was.

The time came when I was to fly the dreaded Beaufighter. 'Dreaded' because the Beaufighter Mk ll had got itself a terrible reputation, especially for swinging about on take-off and landing. The Mk ll differed from all other marks by having Merlin engines. All other marks had Bristol Hercules radial engines, for which the Beau was designed. The Merlin in-line engines were more available at one time and so they were fitted to the Beaus which were held up for power plants. Unfortunately, the marriage was not a great success, making the Mk lls underpowered and at times unmanageable. Apprehension filled our outlook.

To give us some idea of what the Beau was all about, we new pilots were given a demonstration by a pilot of more experience.

We stood in the well behind the driver's seat and looked over his shoulder at what he was doing. I innocently asked for a demonstration of single-engined flying. I wished I hadn't. The demonstrator closed one engine and immediately went into a spiral waltz. He obviously did not enjoy it, neither did I. He quickly powered up the engine again, recovered straight and level flight, landed and disappeared.

A certain amount of cockpit drill was carried out on the ground, until I knew most of the knobs and switches. From that time on I always pictured myself like a cinema organist facing his keyboards, surrounded by dozens of stops, with his feet in the pedals and the seat rising up, as it could in the Beau. The view directly ahead was completely unrestricted - the short, sloping nose arranged that. The side Perspex panels were enormous and came down almost to waist level; this was all right for visibility, but made me feel vulnerable sitting there surrounded by windows.

Doug in his Beaufighter cockpit

The same day as my demonstration flight, I was sent solo. It was my twentieth birthday. Whether I should have considered it a present or not, I was not quite sure. As a fighter, the Beau was vast. I could walk under the nose to the pilot's ladder without bending. All were painted matt black and looked menacing, especially to us. The Merlin engines were set with their tops almost level with the top of the wing; this again gave a good view of everything to the side. I found taxiing so much easier now that I could see what was going on. As soon as I had lined up on the runway and opened both throttles, it was off like a mad animal. I have often seen movie pictures of cowboys riding maddened steers in a rodeo, being bucked about and charging in all directions, and that was exactly how I felt. I knew I was not in control of the beast and hung on tightly, expecting to be thrown off at any time. By the time I had become airborne and had the undercarriage up and was gently climbing, the beast calmed down, so that I thought I might start to enjoy the ride. I remained airborne for an hour, most of the time finding out the feel of the aeroplane and certainly some of the time dreading the moment when I would have to coax this horror back onto the ground. The dry-mouth symptoms of first-solo-itis were ever-present as I offered up the usual prayer to the greatest pilot in the sky, turned onto the final leg, made sure that all vital actions had been dealt with and approached the runway. The beast roared in, happy to think its work for the day was over and it would be returned to its stable. Steve, who was watching from the safety of the flight office, considered it a pretty good landing. I didn't dare tell him that I had done very little towards it.

After a couple more trips on my own in the Beau ll, I was allowed to take Steve with me. His seat was a swivel affair, half-way down the fuselage under a Perspex cupola. While using his radar, by squinting into the visor which surrounded the two cathode ray tubes, he sat facing backwards. When the exercises were over, he could turn round and see, more or less, where we were going. We soon became advanced course members, so were transferred to the satellite 'drome of Winfield, which was slightly nearer to Berwick-on-Tweed. Somehow or other, low flying managed to be indulged in. We thought we were low enough if our slip-stream would ruffle the water on the many small lakes to the north of the aerodrome.

Once, while contour flying in that direction, I saw three figures skylined right at the top of a rise. On closer inspection they appeared to be cardboard cut-outs of soldiers. Targets of some sort, I imagined. If dummy targets, surely we should do a dummy attack. Bringing the Beau up into a steep climb, then heaving over into an equally steep diving turn, I momentarily lost sight of the target, until a few dashes of colour gave me a direction. I just managed to get my sights on to it before pulling up again. In that split second I saw my mistake. I had missed the original figures. My attack had been onto a group of brass hats standing in their staff cars. I could even see their red tabs as they ducked down. The next few minutes, as I flew north hoping they might think I was going home, were filled with mixed emotions. First roaring with laughter, and then great trepidation as to who we'd be hauled up in front of when we eventually got back. Nothing happened at all. I expect the army was too concerned with flattening themselves to even identify which type of aircraft it was, and probably thought it was German anyway.

A dozen more exercises, with three of those being at night, and we were reckoned to be suitably trained to join a squadron. Looking back, I think it was just about as bad as the meagre training of the First World War. We had a few hours on various aircraft admittedly, but the actual training in the techniques of night flying and night fighting using our rather poor radar equipment was a bit skimpy.

Our determination to get as far away from icy Scotland as possible may have prompted our choice of squadron. We were told little and knew little about any squadrons, so a geographical choice was as good as any. Above all, we wanted to be where the action was, and that had to be near to where the enemy came from. 141 Squadron at Ford, near Arundel, on the south coast were short of crews and accepted us.

After a week's leave, most of which was taken up in travelling, we reported to the squadron at Ford, only to find them in a state of chaos in preparation for a move, this time to the Lizard peninsular in Cornwall, to take over the aerodrome at Predannack. I spent one night and two or three meals at Ford. Most of the meal-times were spent under the table, as red warnings were shouted over the Tannoy when F.W.190 fighter bombers screamed in, dropped their single bombs and screamed out again. More elongated train travel to the furthest part of England. The aircraft were flown down by their regular crews, so we had seen neither.

The weather at Predannack was soft, mild and spring-like, almost a complete contrast from our last station. I say 'almost', because the fog must have followed us down. At the drop of a hat, fog could drift in from the sea and envelop the 'drome in a matter of minutes. As it was a very local condition, it was possible to escape to non-fog-bound places within easy reach.

The squadron itself was in the process of being re-formed under its newest commanding officer, Wing Commander Bob Braham. Bob was one of those brilliant pilots who found flying came quite naturally. Standing behind him when he demonstrated the art of beating hell out of the aerodrome, was an experience worth having. On another occasion with me standing behind, he showed great skill by landing in the most shocking conditions with the cloud base very near to the ground. As a night fighter pilot he was almost unsurpassed. His aggression knew no bounds and, although he often admitted to being frightened, his kind of fear was different from anyone else's. His score of victories was mounting and keeping pace with another top night fighter pilot, John Cunningham, yet he was still the youngest wing commander in fighter command.

By the time the war ended, Bob had amassed three D.S.O.s, three D.F.C.s and the Croix de Guerre. By sheer bad luck he ended the war in a prisoner-of-war camp. At the time, I found the squadron morale was at a fairly low ebb, though it had absolutely nothing to do with his leadership, which had not really had time to take effect. Two reasons were, to my way of thinking, responsible for the situation; one the lack of any leave rota, (some crews had gone for months with no time away from the squadron), the second was a lack of action against the enemy. The first was fairly easily remedied and, after a short settling down period, leave started to be available. The second was more difficult. There was a decided lull in the night fighting business. The Luftwaffe was reluctant to fly over England. Raids like the blitz had fizzled out to a great extent. A few loners scurried over and back and were chased by every night fighter in the district. I found little pleasure in patrolling around the Isles of Scilly in the vain hope of something happening. Exercises with friendly targets, although extremely useful, were a half-hearted way to win a war.

Bob Braham, being the aggressive commander he was, sought action of any sort, and I, in my very small way, agreed with him. Most of us tried low-level sweeps down to the Bay of Biscay looking for trouble. We three 141 squadron Beaus would follow three or four coastal command Beaus to the Bay, in the hopes that some kind of enemy would appear. On my patrols, only Spanish fishing boats appeared. I distrusted these as we were sure they were in league with the enemy and radioed any relevant movements of allied ships or aircraft.

My first trip nearly ran us into difficulties, not through any enemy action. The coastal command navigators were supposed to navigate and we to follow. On the way back some bright spark miscalculated the distance and we flew past the tip of Cornwall and headed up the Bristol Channel. Steve knew the chap was wrong from his own navigation, but follow we had to. Eventually we turned back to Predannack, arriving there with everyone shouting about shortages of petrol. Those with the biggest shout landed first. Steve and I, being the lesser mortals, were last in. Again the gauges were reading zero.

I was sent, one morning, across the 'drome to the maintenance hangar to collect a Beau which had had a major inspection and refit and was now ready to be returned to service. Taxiing towards the perimeter track, I was met by a Spitfire that was careering around a blind corner. The inevitable happened. The Spit chewed into the trailing edge of the Beau's wing. I had, at the last moment, tried to take evasive action, but to no avail. The Spitfire's propeller had slashed into the wing right up to the fuselage.

There we were, a great heap of junk. The Station Commander appeared in no time. He was not happy. While inspecting the damage, he was in time to see one of the coastal Beaus just clear the cliffs, crash wheels up onto the runway and catch fire. The poor chap went an awful shade of puce. Two minutes later, yet another coastal Beau crashed onto the field with obvious hydraulic trouble. It was too much for the poor chap. He literally jumped up and down on the spot, shouting rude words and other things like 'Get them off'. I never knew what he meant; maybe he did.

The coastal Beaus had met a very persistent Ju 88 meteorological aircraft and, in trying to shoot it down, had come up against a very good, and very brave, air-gunner who sat there shooting and hitting the Beaus as they attacked. The burning Beaus became a hazard when the ammunition started exploding.

The Spitfire pilot got into awful trouble for speeding and for not looking where he was going - a very difficult thing to do, if you have a long way to taxi in a Spitfire. You can't see where you are going and it boils if you take too long.

FIRST 'OP'

Low level at night in my clapped out Beau
On the train line from St Brieuc to Brest
The hazy half moon tried hard to show
The rails running from east to the west

It was my first 'op' my very first 'op'
And I guess I was still very keen
My job that night was to clobber and stop
Any railway train there to be seen

We could follow the rails by the glint on the track
So follow, we did, mile after mile
Not a puff of smoke all there and back
Not a movement for all of the while

Some guns at Morlaix sent a burst of 'ack ack'
Looked like a small firework show
I thought it a pretty pathetic attack
The shells bursting far left and below

We blundered along, up and down the straight line
Not a thing did we see all the way
I thought there and then, it a great waste of time
So we knew it was pointless to stay

We got back home, brassed off and irate
Having pursued such a time-wasting flight
'If that's ops,' I thought, 'It's a right sorry state
To be prowling around half the night.'

We got into de-brief and tried to complain
That the night was not what was planned
The intelligence officer then tried to explain
And he hoped that we might understand

Unknown to us, some six hours before
The French Maquis had been up to their tricks
So the viaduct at Morlaix was no more
Just an enormous pile of bricks

Later I thought 'ops' a right piece of cake
There's nothing to get worried about
Soon I learned I was wrong, for God's sake
Not long after, I was to find out.

My next trip of interest occurred during the time that Steve was in the sick bay enjoying measles. Two Beaus, mine being one, were to pop across to Brittany on a moonlight night, follow the coastal railway around the Morlaix district and blow up any trains which appeared. It was a pity that no-one had told us that some fighter-bombers had blown up the line that very afternoon so that no trains could run anyway - hence no trains and no action on my part. It was a nice trip apart from my first baptism of flak, which I didn't care much for, even though it missed by a mile. Leaving the French coast by Le Mont St. Michel was fun, as I'd visited it by bus only a few years before. It looked very different by moonlight. While Steve was still coping with his measles, I crewed with some odd navigator who had no pilot at that moment. He, I believe, could have had little imagination, so suffered my flying without comment.

One unusual trip we flew together was an air-sea-rescue mission. A Lancaster bomber had been ditched a few miles off the French coast - at least, it was nearer the French coast than the English, somewhere off Finisterre. Two or three of us Beaus plus a few Spitfires were to give cover in case the enemy tried to get there first. The Lancaster was perfectly ditched, floating with the whole of the top of the wing clear of the water. The water itself was dead flat, apart from a slight swell. A great fluorescent scar changed the surrounding sea a bright yellowish-green colour and was visible for miles. The crew sat patiently in their round dinghy. The whole operation was absolutely copybook. I overtook the RAF rescue boat skimming out from Falmouth. A Walrus amphibian aircraft arrived on the scene. We fighters milled around for over two hours watching the rescue, with not a sign from the enemy. Some of the Lancaster's crew got home by Walrus and some by launch.

A couple of years ago I was having a cup of tea in the cafe in the RAF Museum at Hendon, and sitting opposite me was an oldish chap wearing an RAF tie with small motifs on it which I'd not seen before. I asked him what it was and was told that it was the air-sea-rescue tie. During the ensuing conversation, we discovered that we had both been on that Lancaster rescue all those years before, he in the rescue boat and me up above.

Our time at Predannack was useful in-so-far as it brought the Squadron to a much better frame of mind. Some crew members disappeared because they didn't fit, some lost in action, and one by sheer overconfidence and incompetence on the part of the pilot. I have always maintained that if you must show off by buzzing the 'drome at low level, look at what you are doing and not at the people on the ground, who might be waving or lying flat. He didn't, and let his wing-tip hit a Tannoy speaker stuck up on a pole. The Beau flicked into the ground. I watched all this from above; it was horrible. I helped carry the box of the unfortunate navigator to his grave.

A move was rumoured, and a change of job. The object was to go to the enemy if he would not come to us. Bomber Command's heavies were having a pretty terrible time sustaining mounting losses over Germany, to what was becoming unacceptable numbers. Our new job was to try to do something about it by chasing off the German fighters. By careful research into the equipment carried by the German night fighters, their working frequencies were found. A black box was made for us, which gave us the ability to home onto that frequency, then coupled with our antiquated radar, we might be able to chase them up. Our boffins had been very clever, and after inspecting a German Ju 88 which had accidentally landed in England, they created a device called 'Serrate'. Serrate because of the jagged trace on the cathode ray tube - one more thing for the radar operator to watch. Unfortunately it was an elementary piece of gubbins, which gave direction of the German, but not his range. If facing us, the signal strength was quite powerful but might be miles away; if on the beam, the signal might give the impression of being far away when really he was quite close.

The German operators had a bad habit of only turning their radar sets on for a comparatively short time, probably because the sets suffered from overheating. This, of course, restricted the time we had to find where he was and develop the chase. If we were not careful, we could find ourselves chasing contacts all over the sky and getting nowhere. The standard practice was to keep following a strong signal and if it vanished to keep on in that direction in the hope that it would appear again. If it did, well and good, if not, one would end up miles off course and probably lost.

For this new venture we moved to Wittering, in Northamptonshire - a lovely aerodrome with grass runways and joining up with Collyweston, a smaller airfield next to us, giving us the length of two aerodromes. In those days the Great North Road ran past the guardroom entrance. We were within walking distance from the multi-pubbed town of Stamford. I should say walking distance there and staggering distance back. It was on this road that I had a very near shave, and nothing to do with the enemy or aeroplanes. I had just left the main gate on my way out of camp, preparing to cycle to Stamford, when I met, waiting at the bus stop just outside the gate, a W.A.A.F. She was actually an acquaintance of Steve's. I can't remember her name, but I do recall that she was beautiful enough to stop and talk to. Straddling my bike and leaning across the handlebars seemed a comfortable and informal way to chat. By some quirk of fate I happened to glance behind me and in that split second noticed the front wheels of an approaching lorry begin to wobble. The ancient driver lost control and I was in line to be written off. I just had time to scoot a couple of feet forward before this heap mounted the pavement, brushed my back wheel and crashed into the ditch. I think the lorry's track rods were some way back along the road, leaving the driver, whose life's blood was oozing all over the shattered windscreen, with a freely rotating steering wheel. All at the bus stop were so concerned to make sure that the poor chap stayed in this world, that none at the time realised how near the incident was to mass slaughter. I thought afterwards, 'Who needs the enemy?' and 'Whatever would my Mum have said if I'd been killed in action with a lorry?'

I had not been on the squadron all that long, in training for our new job on 'Serrate' operations, chasing around Germany looking for the German night fighters, when we were given the name 'Bomber Support Special Duties Squadron'. I felt that being such a distinguished title, I as a mere Sergeant Pilot would learn more of the workings of the complicated job, if I was to become a commissioned officer and be a little closer to the source of the things we were supposed to do. This, I felt, would also be an asset for my navigator, so we both applied for commissions. Navigators originally in our business were called an 'RO' or radar operator. The 'RO' brevett was soon changed to 'N' for navigator, in case they were shot down and captured and the Gestapo brought out the thumb-screws to glean any information about the secrets of 'Serrate'". As if they didn't already know. Until we were fully trained we were still sat waiting for any Huns trespassing over England, though by then that was becoming a more and more occasional adventure for them. Their main job was to protect their own home land from our bombers, which were knocking Hell out of their pretty towns.

On one supposedly quiet evening, we in the Sergeants' Mess were having a 'do'. All the officers would make a point of being there, as the WAAFs would be much more available and friendly. A few of we underling Sergeants would be placed on night duty and stand by to chase away any incoming raiders. We waited in the crew-room while all the others were enjoying our boozy party. All of a sudden some idiot German was reported to be in our airspace, way up in the North of England. "Scramble, scramble," and all that film-star rubbish, in no time we were aboard our Beaufighter and heading north. It was not a nice night for going anywhere, and at 20,000 feet it was cold and miserable. Quite why the Beaufighter's heater was so poor I never discovered. Prowling around somewhere near the Firth of Forth we stooged around for ages, until eventually the controller said it was a Halifax bomber on some kind of cross-country flight and we could go home. I was totally fed up. Back home we flew, still cursing the loss of the party in the mess.

Returning to our aerodrome we found the circuit cluttered up with banks of fog, especially at lower altitudes. Turning onto finals I became enveloped in a great bank of un-see-through-able stuff, so I quickly stuck the nose down to get below it. What a pity I had not gone through the pre-landing checks which included ensuring that the guns, all ten of them, had been set to Safe. BANG-BANG-BANG-BANG – what a racket! I thought I was being fired on by all the Huns in creation. Oh dear, almost immediately I knew it was me, pushing hard on the stick I had gripped the firing button and set off the blessed artillery. I landed and could hear the air-raid sirens sounding off in the nearest town. My flight commander thought the whole thing hilarious, especially as I'd managed to blow a hangar door off its runners. And so to bed.

Next day, a different kind of hell was let loose. The Engineer Officer was furious about my escapades of the previous night. He was a chap whose whole world was black and who hated everyone and everything to do with nasty little sergeants. It was said of him that he needed no telephone, when he made a call, his shouting could be heard even on long-distance calls. I have forgotten exactly what he said, but it was then I discovered I was illegitimate.

The final insult was when my application for a commission was turned down. This was not because I'd blown the hangar door off, but because I hadn't passed my matriculation exam. Six months later, all was forgiven when a new Commanding Officer reckoned we deserved our commissions and Steve and I were made Pilot Officers.

There was a final act to this story. Many years later when Steve was having a drink in a bar in Berkhamsted, he heard a chap telling how he had been in that very same hangar with some WAAF – laying down I believe – when the heel of his boot was blown off by some twit in a Beaufighter. Did Steve tell him? I don't know.

I have been told that every Squadron has at least one "Bloody Fool" within its complement. I'm afraid I qualified for that title in mine.

After a month of stooging around Wittering and taking part in unproductive night exercises, we were packed off to Drem for a week's special training in the art of using Serrate. Drem was a much nicer place in the early summer than the last time I'd been there in the middle of winter. The idea of using Scotland as a training area was that, being so far from the enemy, the earth's curvature would make it impossible for them to twig what we were doing by listening to our V.H.F. chatter, or our use of odd frequencies. The week at Drem, plus another intense training at Wittering, using our interception methods by day and night, gave us some idea of how things worked. By mid-June I was considered to be practised enough to fly over enemy territory. How different reality turned out to be.

Nazis and Mosquitos.

It is not fashionable, these days, to talk of hate. Hate is an emotion to be suppressed, the same as the wish to destroy. In the nineteen-forties I hated with a deep-seated hatred. I wished to destroy with all the power I could muster. I hated the Nazis. I hated their creed, their swastika, their arrogance, their cruelty. I hated everything about them, and I had an overwhelming desire to destroy them. We all knew enough about their policies of extermination, their boastings of the master race. We'd all seen the struttings of their leaders and the homage of their underlings. I hated the whole rotten lot. Sometime later, after visiting Dachau, I knew I had been right. Somehow this Third Reich had to be destroyed. If one or two pretty German cities were sacrificed, that was just one of the small penalties to be paid. If the civilian population in Germany suffered the allied bombing, I assume they were the ones we'd seen in newsreels, welcoming Hitler with 'Sieg Heils' and Nazi salutes every time he appeared.

They, with the military, were only too pleased to jeer, stone, oppress and murder anyone not of their creed. Let's not kid ourselves that the Nazis were a small minority of the German race. The small percentage who were opposed to the regime had either left in the thirties or were keeping very quiet. Of course, when I visited Germany just after the war, not a Nazi was to be found anywhere. Even the overfed thugs of guards, whom I had seen sunbathing at Dachau awaiting denazification or trial, declared they only acted under orders and didn't like what they were told to do. Many thinking people had the same outlook as myself and many were determined to do something about it. I believe we all knew what we were fighting for, and what would happen if the Nazis took over.

To digress, after the war, while waiting for the American Air Force to fly us to England in one of their many Dakotas, we had a look around what was left of Munich. Mostly it was great piles of burnt and fallen masonry, stacked up so as to leave the road clear for traffic to pass. Some parts of the city, however, were only slightly marked by bombing. I remember having coffee in one of the grand Nazi arenas, which was still standing, its white concrete almost unmarked.

We transiting airmen lived in a newly-built wooden mess, very comfortable with its triple-glazed windows. 'Happy Hour', an expression I had never met before, meant that all, or nearly all, the booze was free for that short time, encouraging all-comers to get as much 'down' as possible.

If we were to travel anywhere outside the mess or aerodrome, it was in a three-ton lorry, usually an open vehicle, but here the back was covered by a canvas sheet and there were benches on the floor. We were advised not to sit with the benches at the edge so our backs would have rested against the canvas side as the Germans had a habit of slashing the canvas with sharp knives in the hope of killing us passengers. The RAF lorries were particularly vulnerable. I was not surprised, we remembered Hitler had used Munich as one of his propaganda platforms, it was full of Nazi sympathisers, and the RAF had messed it up a bit.

One morning we heard that a number of Americans were to visit Dachau, the concentration camp, which was only a few miles from our HQ, so we went along as well. Inside this death camp there was an all-pervading feeling of gloom. Miserable wooden huts scattered around in a dilapidated condition gave it a look of neglect. We met and talked to a few of the American doctors, who were among the first to enter the place. They said they could smell the camp long before they entered, yet the Germans living in the vicinity insisted they knew nothing of what was going on in this so-called 'hospital'". It's difficult to see how they could equate the arrival of so many degraded 'patients' when no one ever left. I stood inside one of the gas chambers, but could hardly imagine the horrors which had gone on there.

With typical German thoroughness, all the victims were documented, either before or after being trolleyed into the furnaces to be disposed of. Experiments of various sorts were carried out in the laboratories, and I had time to read some of the translated notes. One experiment, which obviously affected me, was the business of plunging prisoners into ice-cold sea water to find out how long they might survive wearing various uniforms and flying suits. They also carried out experiments on whether reviving them was possible, placing a very cold man in bed with a warm woman was one method tried, with, I can only suppose, some chap standing there with a stop-watch. Lines of glass jars held bits and pieces of human remains, only, I suppose, what you might find in any hospital, but I wondered how they got there. I will not continue with the description of more horrible sights, I will only say that there are some who say it never happened.

Man's inhumanity to man has, I imagine, been going on since Cain and Abel, but the Nazi concentration camps must have been some of the most awful. Visiting the city of Munich again in the last few years is an amazing experience, to find such a beautiful place with no sign of the past atrocities. Are the modern population as beautiful, I wonder?

Pre ops, pre take-off

Concrete crewroom, chilly damp
Mae West too tight round my waist
Oh God, make the weather clamp
Coffee's got an awful taste.

Dry mouth, dry throat, straining eyes
Mozzie waiting in the dark
Steve had registered surprise
At the Wing Co's grim remark.

Courses plotted, watches set
Nearly ready for the show
Got the latest gen. from met.
O.K. Steve, it's time to go.

Very many pilots of distinction have written of their combat experiences, to such an extent that possibly we all have read just about everything. I have marvelled at their, exploits, been jealous of their scores of kills, been astounded by their bravery, and so assured that my own contribution made such a small impression on the course and outcome of the war as to deserve only a passing mention. In our two tours of operations flown over enemy territory, Steve and I found out what it was like to be continuously coned by searchlights, peppered and thumped by lumps of flak, chased by foes and friends, shot at by anyone who had a gun handy and generally frightened stiff.

On our credit side, we must have kept an awful lot of Germans awake, frightened quite a lot, chased a number and killed a few. All of our operational flights were hazardous, for us and the enemy. Radar on both sides was in its infancy; in my case I only had to hear the swearing and see the green flashes around Steve's department to know that the set was about to blow up or had already done so. This would either happen as we almost had a Hun in range or when we were hundreds of miles from home and feeling defenceless. It was not a good feeling to find the radar had packed up, when we were, usually, unsure of our position and then, by accident, cross the stream of dozens of heavy bombers. If they saw us, they'd fire. If we didn't see them, we'd hit their slipstream and be tossed all over the sky. When we did see them, they looked enormous and menacing.

Our forward-looking radar nearly always suffered with a squint, giving an incorrect indication which could, with skill, be overcome until things got complicated like trying to see behind, where the normal forward radar could see a little way, but in reverse. Before every operation we flew a night flying test, usually in the early afternoon. During this time the radar was checked for efficiency, squint or anything else which might have to be overcome by Steve that night. The test gave me the opportunity to try the aeroplane in various phases of flight - single-engined flying, limited instrument flying, general instrument flying especially on one engine, mock attacks and a bit of sheer enjoyment of flying a powerful aeroplane made the afternoon test a real treat.

1944

The terror night unfolds at nightmare pace
The chase, so long and menacingly slow
The bandit blip creeps down the radar trace
The shadowed stalking of the hated foe.

The night sky cloaks the deadly game
This hide and seek is only for the skilled
No right, no wrong, no rules, no blame,
Just kill, or you'll be killed.

Then in the ring-sight ghostly shapes emerge
Quite unmistakeable, that black silhouette
And stealthily the dread machines converge
The range diminishes, the guns are set.

The writhing agony, the searing rape
Swastika arrogances have swiftly died
The blazing mess spins in its evil shape
To leave the sky disgorged and purified.

All glamour left behind us on the ground
The Brylcream and bravado doesn't show
The cordite, sweat and petrol all around
Are not the things the public wants to know.

Merlins running roughly, grinding home
War over for tonight and left behind
Beacon flashing, beckons to our aerodrome
Relief and weariness are now combined.

The torn wing is evidence of fight
The staggering craft hangs limply in the air
Our circuit lights become a welcome sight
We see our friendly runway waiting there.

Later, at the evening briefing we learned where we would be going and what we would be expected to do. On entering the briefing room we would sit and wait for the large map on the wall to be unveiled to show us the coloured ribbons tracing our routes. Forced humour attacked most of us as we joked about the miles of enemy territory we would have to cover, or how the flak was the last time we went that way. The met. man nearly always had a 'low' somewhere up his sleeve. His weather pictures covered the whole of our routes, sometimes good, often terrible. I have known him to say that we could go, but it would be unlikely if we'd be able to get back. A more detailed picture of the raid - the number of bombers, spoofs, diversionary targets, markers, turning points for the main force, the expected opposition, German fighter bases, lengths of time in the target area, and many more relevant details, and of course the part we were to play in all this - was explained by the Wing Commander. Times for our take-off were noted. Navigators worked out the routes. Escape kits were drawn. Then the night-flying supper - just like the prisoner having his last hearty meal before the off. Then we'd be off to the crew room to get dressed and ready. A few minutes before take-off we would climb aboard our aeroplane, close the hatch and pull the darkness around us.

It was a mistake to think that the night protected anyone. We were there to show the Germans that it did not, I hoped. It was not always the case, as on the night, when, after struggling to climb a clapped-out Beau to our operating height, I could only manage to coax it to fourteen thousand feet. As we were approaching the Dutch coast, Steve quietly requested a slight turn to the left, as he had a hazy contact, but couldn't be sure whether it was in front or behind. Almost immediately my reverie was shattered by Steve shouting the one word 'Christ'. In that thousandth of a second I knew, first that Steve, not being terribly religious, had been really goaded into action and second, that I must at least equal that action. I pushed the controls frantically in to the left-hand corner, and the aircraft responded by flicking onto its back and descending rapidly just giving me time to see, what Steve must have seen when he had glanced up from his visor. The multi-gunned enemy was hosing away at point-blank range. The brightness of his cannon obliterated his silhouette, so that I could not identify the aircraft. He couldn't possibly miss, but he did. If the roles had been reversed, I wouldn't have missed. All my instruments that could topple, did topple. I could hear the Beau creaking and groaning as I tried to pull out from the dive. Steve said we were making vapour trails like a corkscrew. Eventually I watched the airspeed coming down past the three hundred and ninety mark and, in the light of the moon's last quarter, saw the sea racing up to meet us. As I heaved hard back on the stick, the nose started to indicate a climb, so that by the time I had the thing more or less under control, we were at three thousand feet. I thought at the time, 'This is definitely not what it's all about. I thought I was supposed to do the chasing and shooting.' I have wondered since, what happened when the roles did become reversed? Did they have time to call on the Almighty? So the ability to see backwards, using our radar was a help, even though the range was extremely limited.

Some wonder-man, at the Ministry, even suggested we allowed the enemy fighter to sneak up on us and just when he thought we were a sitter, to go into a steep turn until we were on his tail. He should have tried it. The radar was not that good. Nevertheless, it was of some comfort when on one occasion we were slap over Berlin, the searchlights waited until they had us where they wanted us then, all of a sudden, exposed hundreds of shafts of light. We were trapped. The cockpit was like icy daylight. This was no new experience, but the cones were a little more concentrated than usual. First I tried to weave out of the light. My contortions were of no avail and when I realised I'd almost started to fly back the way I'd come, I settled down to straight and level flying. No flak came up, making me sure we were being followed. No radar contacts behind. It felt scary just because nothing was happening. Ten very long minutes elapsed before we flew out of range of those awful lights. I've often wondered what they thought they were doing; normally they were so thorough with their lights and fighters.

As we often flew completely alone and away from the bomber stream, we would have any flak that was going all to ourselves. The great barrages sent up to greet us, were, fortunately, fairly inaccurate, sometimes exploding well above and raining down on our heads, sometimes slightly below, giving us a kick in the seat. Speed came to our rescue so that, when we flew the Mosquitoes, we would fly ourselves out of trouble. Predicted flak was different. If you could pin-point the flak battery which was firing at you, and sometimes you could see the gun flashes on the ground, then, by counting off the seconds, you could time the bursts. If too close, a thirty degree change of course, held for the same number of seconds, would put you into a position to watch for the burst to appear off to one side. Change course and wait again. Continue with an unpredictable pattern of course changes and hope the gunners below were not too bright. It didn't work every time. If above cloud, cross your fingers, pray and take your chance. I still have a souvenir from Paris, which came with the very first burst of flak and hit my aeroplane just below my seat. Made me jump at the time.

Lucky for some

It was warmer in the cockpit than outside in the rain
And when the hatch was closed we were in our own domain
With engines primed, the switches on, the throttles eased apart
We waited for the erk to give his thumbs up sign to start

Starboard first and then the port, the Merlins coughed and roared
But somehow things seemed 'not quite right' to both of us on board
The taxi track, ill lit with blue dots, filtered through the gloom
Gave Steve and I a sense of fear, foreboding, creeping doom

Positioned at the runway's end, the green flash bade us go
But still this deepening apprehension stayed, forecasting woe
The take-off steady, straight and true, then black as black the night
She clawed her way, a straining way, grasping for more height

Then into thick unfriendly cloud, which broke at fourteen thou
To find the brilliant moonlight, which had been hidden up to now
So on and on till the target's fire assured the track O.K.
The flack was light, the searchlights dead, dense cloud had killed their play

Our long patrol toiled on and on, and still no bandit blip
But yet some worry nagged and nagged all this unholy trip
The long haul back, uneasy, fearful, tiring and hard
And even on our circuit we kept forever on our guard

We bounded down the runway still half concealed by rain
And headed for the dispersal torches guiding us again
Not until we'd stuffed ourselves with grub, after the debrief
Did we allow our thoughts to show a blessed great relief

We both now knew why our fears came quickly to a stop
We both thanked god we had survived our dreaded thirteenth op.

Having mentioned Mosquitoes, I had better say how we got them. Got *them*, is not quite right. We, that is the squadron, got one. It arrived one day, and there it was. The top people flew it. After a while it appeared to be left around and my flight commander suggested that I flew it. We had had the 'pilot's notes', little books with most of the information concerning the business of flying the aeroplane in it, for a day or two. After climbing in, settling into my seat, adjusting the foot pedals, touching all the controls and finding out where things were and what things did, I knew I was going to like it. Starting up, taxiing out, taking off, and it got better and better. I thought it the most wonderful aeroplane I had ever flown. I still do. Landing was easy compared with the Beau, and it stayed straight.

A Mosquito

At the time I described it as a twin-engined Tiger Moth. Even though the Mosquitoes we were given were old, they were gorgeous. Steve sat next to me, not like the Beau, where he sat down the back and faced the wrong way round. The heater worked, not like the Beau, where my left shoe got burnt but my hands and face froze.

Operational flying continued, sometimes in the Beau; sometimes, and as more arrived, often in Mosquitoes. Each trip to enemy country presented new experiences, some bad, some not so bad: the sight of burning cities, red with bursts of high explosive bombs and seething with unstoppable incendiaries cascading down in their thousands so that the whole expanse gave the impression of incandescent erupting and boiling toffee; the pangs of dismay when watching a Lancaster flaming down in its death dive and trying not to imagine what was going on inside; the helplessness of seeing a great bomber, coned by hundreds of searchlights, unable to extricate itself from the deadly web of beams, until the pursuing fighters killed it.

Chases using 'Serrate' became less frequent, as the German boffins realised what we were doing and consequently made frequency changes and generally improved their radar capabilities. Chases were sometimes brought to the ultimate conclusion. I hadn't realised till then, how when an aircraft is shattered by the full blast of four twenty millimetre cannon, it stops flying, like a shot pheasant, only, in the case of an aeroplane, it spews burning lumps of itself backwards. Violent evasive action was necessary to avoid being clobbered by the smoking debris. If the enemies' hydraulic system was shot away and the undercarriage fell down, the target slowed to such an extent that, again, quick action was called for, or it was only too easy to run into the back of it. A hard-climbing turn usually solved the problem, and then you could watch and wait for the explosion on the ground, which would light up the sky for miles.

The hot-blooded dog-fight of the day fighter was not our method of combat. Ours was a slow, calculated stalking of the enemy; creeping up on the target, close enough for positive identification and by then, too close for the firing, allowing the enemy, in all his ignorance to extend the range a little, pull up until the dimmed ring sight enclosed the silhouette, hold the breath and squeeze the firing button.

Surprisingly, some parts of operational flying compensated for the awful times. I can recall on several occasions, leaving the enemy coast just as dawn was breaking, watching the sky change from hostile blackness to soft mother-of-pearl, and then the welcoming water-colours of the English countryside in early light, or the sight of Lincoln Cathedral emerging through morning mist, or even the red flashing beacon of one's own aerodrome. After landing, Steve would come out from his transfixed radar gaze, look at me, and say, "We've fooled him again" - 'him' being the devil, and we being still alive.

Doug after the award of his D.F.C. in 1944

Engines

Oh yes, I remember when the nights were far too long
When the dreaded moon rose slowly cruel and vengeful
And we all felt the biting, nagging chill was fearful
As we listened so closely to the Merlin's song

Then struggling to the upper air where sanity had gone
Heaving hard and climbing through the grasping cloud
And hearing, all the time, strange noises over loud
As we concentrated solely on the Merlin's song

The gauges, never moving, declaimed there's nothing wrong
With the engines grinding to a steady drumming drum
And keeping up their invading throbbing hum
But still we listened acutely to the Merlin's song

Nearing our objective we're wide awake and strong
Nerves keyed to a heightened tension, strain
And as soon as it was possible, bang the power on again
And never fail to heed the roaring Merlin's song

Remember, yes I remember all this time along
Through fear and sheer determination
We bored our way regardless through the deflagration
As we listened more intently to the Merlin's song

I'll not forget, though many many years have gone
How the reek of oil and sweat still lingers yet
As then, so now, nothing ever to regret
We came to love the mighty Merlin's song

At the time I could see no good reason to be rested from the squadron. It had become my way of life after the twenty-two months I had been there. I felt nothing else existed, especially as, although D-Day was past and the war looked as though we might eventually win, there was still a long way to go and I wanted to stay with it. Admittedly, at least twenty-six crews had been lost somehow or other during our time on the squadron. Some missing, some prisoners of war, some just lost and never heard of again, and one or two lost for a while until they walked back. One Belgian crew in particular took only about ten days to get from being shot down in Holland to arriving at Gibraltar. Steve and I felt that so far we had been lucky and wondered how long that situation would last.

Eventually, we were told officially that our rest was overdue and, very decently, I thought, asked what job we would like to do in the future. Naturally, Steve and I would like a job where we would still fly as a team. I suggested that, instead of the usual, going back to O.T.U. to instruct lesser pilots and navigators into the ways of night fighting, we might be found a job where any skills we might have, could be used to test aeroplanes and Radars. I even suggested a posting to the Air Force's test establishment at Boscombe Down, where I had made a visit a few months before and had seen some of the interesting capers that were being tried out. After enquiries, I was told that no vacancies existed and for the moment Steve and I would go to Cranfield to instruct at the O.T.U.

I had realised earlier on that one of the great pleasures in aviation was, as far as I was concerned, the business of trying out different and varied types of aircraft. The armament officer at Wittering had loaned me his Miles Master ll, a brilliant little aeroplane. Wonderful for aerobatics. Wonderful for stirring up the adrenalin. Easy to fly, even easier to fly badly. An aeroplane with enough vices to command great respect. Its near relation, the target-towing Martinet, I found, was not anything like as much fun, especially when towing a drogue so that the squadron Mosquitoes could shoot at it. After a few three-hour stints in the Martinet, I realised I should not have volunteered to fly it.

A short time before my adventures as a target-tower, a Bolton and Paul Defiant arrived on the squadron for use as a radar target. I couldn't resist trying it for size. I flew it on many occasions and could quite see why, in the Battle of Britain, my squadron had been massacred on one afternoon when their Defiants met a force of determined Me 109's. With no fixed, forward-firing guns, but only a power turret of four machine guns swinging around behind, the pilot of the Defiant stood little chance against a highly manoeuvrable single-seat fighter. A pleasant enough creature to fly, but never a day fighter. I seem to remember that the pneumatic braking system was not too good. I ended up stuck in the mud trying to taxi around West Raynham at night. Even when I had been extricated and got airborne, the pressure failed to build up and I diverted to Wittering's long grass runway. I seem to think also that I never quite figured out the odd fuel system where one tank drained into another by pressing buttons.

A couple of dear old Ansons were stationed with us for a while. They were as docile as big shaggy dogs. I felt I needed a bus driver's hat while flying them. Steve hated them. He had to wind up the undercarriage by hand. It took a lot of turns to raise it, sitting almost sideways and living with the knowledge that in no time at all, the process of winding it down again was not far away.

The squadron hack, at one time, was a Miles Magister, yet another delight. This little low-winged two-seater was a basic trainer but, unlike the Tiger Moth, could be flown solo from the front seat. From the front, with only the bonnet housing the engine, the view was excellent. No wires or top wing like the Tiger. Rather like driving an airborne sports car. A favourite pastime of mine was to fly along the East Anglian dykes with the wheels just above the stream and the wings level with the banks. I had on occasion taken it home to Wiltshire in an afternoon, and then returned early next morning, driving the whole way at low altitude. That was terrific.

One memorable day at Cranfield, I discovered a Beaufort sitting on the tarmac. After enquiries, I was told it was to be taken to Filton, but that no-one was available to fly it there. Being foolish and rushing in, I volunteered to do so; after all, I had flown three marks of Bristol Blenheim and three marks of Beaufighter. I only needed the Beaufort to complete my Bristol Aircraft set. The knobs and switches were distributed in the usual Bristol fashion, visibility was limited through its stained-glass windows and it was raining at the time. The whole contraption shook and shuddered with aerial ague. Maybe this Beaufort was particularly old and certainly clapped out, but climb it would not. Throughout the journey I could not coax it above fifteen hundred feet. The controls felt like a wooden spoon in an uncooked Christmas pudding. On my arrival at Filton, the chief in the hangar said, "It's here to be scrapped."

With all the sixteen or so different aircraft I had flown by that time, I realised that during the first few flights, one was not only testing one's own ability to manage them, but evaluating their particular qualities. If flown to their, and my, maximum capabilities, a good deal of knowledge and satisfaction was to be gained. Also, the comparison of one aircraft with another of the same type could indicate where slight improvements might be made.

The RAF has had a great tradition of adding bits and pieces to aeroplanes since the word go. What starts as a beautifully smooth and streamlined creation soon finds it is lumbered with extras in the form of fuel tanks, aerials, funny noses, lumps and bumps covering all manner of necessary after-thoughts, guns, rockets and rails, bombs, more and bigger tanks, more bumps and bulges, until the poor thing has a Christmas tree look with all the bits hung on. We had our fair share and experience of this with all our extra radar gubbins, so that evaluation of the type became second nature. This kind of thing, I thought, might be the job of the test pilot and I would like to have something to do with it.

Strange as it might seem, the next job for Steve and me, after a very short stint at Cranfield and Twinwoods O.T.U. North of Bedford (the airfield from which Glenn Miller flew and was never seen again) was to co-operate with another service who had been hanging lumps, bumps, aerials and what-have-you onto their particular fighting machine. The Royal Navy needed our help. Testing of radar equipment was to take place, to evaluate the capabilities of the latest long range, very large, Battle Class Destroyer *Barfleur*. This beautiful ship was to spend three months at Gibraltar, during which time her radar was to be tried out against dummy attacks by aircraft.

Steve and I were to be in one of the aircraft, a brand new Mosquito straight from the Standard Motor factory. We were to pick it up at Melton Mowbray, test it, and then fly to Gibraltar.

During the whole of my flying career I have only flown two brand-new aeroplanes; one was that Mosquito, the other was my S.E.5a.

CHAPTER ELEVEN
September 16th 1987 – first flight

There had been times in the past, when I have sat in the cockpit and have said, sometimes out loud, "What am I doing here?" I have wondered why, of all the various things I could have done in the world, I had to choose aviation. Why not golf, or stamp collecting, or anything else where one could grow old gracefully and with less expense? I can remember from war-time days thinking, 'Why couldn't I stay sitting in the security of an office?' After all, that was what I'd been doing for ages. Why stick one's neck out? Flying out over blacked-out East Anglia, I used to picture the people down below going up to their snug and safe beds, while I headed for Germany. Why couldn't I be like them? I have met many war-time pilots since who have declared that they would be happy never to see another aeroplane again, yet, there was I, and here I still am, trying like mad to clamber into the air at every chance, even though, at times past, I knew I was not going to enjoy it. I can no more explain this urgent feeling than can anyone else who is driven by some incomprehensible force to follow or chase their particular calling.

Air-mindedness in England has never caught on, at least, not in a big way. Yes, we like to think of the Battle of Britain, rather as we think of the Spanish Armada, Yes, we like to go to air displays and watch and hope we're never asked to join in. Way back in the past, when I was a boy at school, I can remember being the only member of my class who had flown, and that included the form-master. Five years before, when I left teaching, things had changed little. Some children had flown to a holiday resort, but none had ever been in a small aeroplane, and didn't want to. In my young days I was a member of the Air League of the British Empire. I wonder what happened to that. We know what happened to the British Empire; maybe the League went the same way.

My mother and father were both keen on flying. All my horrible aunts and uncles, of whom there were dozens, wouldn't have gone near to an aeroplane if they were paid. People of my age have welcomed the motor-car as a friend, when it is, or can be, a potential killer of great numbers of road users, but will only travel in Jumbo Jets with their teeth gritted and a large swig of brandy, plus all the while thinking how wonderful some smelly foreign holiday spot will be if they ever get there. Thank goodness a lot of the younger generation know better. They have found hang-gliding and micro-light planes and are willing to step off into the unknown.

Des ready to swing the propeller

In the five or six minutes of warming up the S.E.5a, more thoughts came into my mind. Here I was after four years' struggle, with the plane all finished and ready. All those people who had helped me to get this far, this was for them as well as me. What about those who thought it wouldn't work? What about the teacher who said, "He's building his own coffin." Thoughts crowded into my brain and vanished again when I insisted on thinking positively.

I knew the aeroplane was perfectly O.K. After all, I'd spent a lot of time getting it right. The measurements were right, the incidence was right, the C of G was right. The engine was running well. Damn it, I had flown plenty of aeroplanes before, some of which I'd known very little about. This was different - I'd brought this one into the world, stick by stick, bracket by bracket. It looked good and it felt good and I felt at home in it. It fitted. My feet and hands made contact in the right places. I felt comfortable.

Doug ready for take-off on the first flight in his SE5a

I waved the chocks away, taxied a few yards along the grass, turned into wind and slowly pushed the throttle to the wide open position. Life flowed through the whole aeroplane. The tail lifted as the speed increased. This creature was just so eager to get into its element. All my intentions of fast taxi runs vanished. It wanted to fly, so who was I to say no? It became a living thing. It was no longer an 'it'. She positively bounded along the grass and with a skittish hop clung to the air, as if on tip-toe, then reached upward. There was no need to consciously move any controls. I thought her into climb and into the turns. We were both happy.

It was then down to business. Check temperatures and pressures. Check engine revs. Climb to a reasonable height and check the stalling speed. Would she fly hands off? All was well, maybe a small adjustment on the trim tab would take the small amount of weight off the stick at cruising speed.

Take-off!
Doug's son, Steve, watching

So far I had been too taken up with the thrill of flying to even look down at the small group of helpers below. A low run over them must have convinced them that all was well. I could see Des hurrying back to the hangar to board the club's Jodel aircraft, to join me in the sky. I tried a few steep turns, gliding turns and side-slips while waiting for the Jodel to join me. We flew in formation long enough for a quick photographic record to be made of the first flight. The landing was not difficult. I had noted the angle of the nose against the horizon before take-off, so brought the aeroplane to within a few feet of the ground, At just above the stall, she gently brushed her wheels along the grass, before settling down onto the ground. The date was the 16th of September 1987 and I was happy.

After putting the aeroplanes away and closing up the hangar, we celebrated with a glass of champagne, before making our way home. I spent a fortune that night telephoning all who had helped in any way to make flying my S.E.5a possible, to tell the good news.

It was some little time before the realisation completely sank in. I had achieved it. Not entirely alone, I was the first to admit, but I had started this project and had seen it through. No, I was not proud. I think pride, if it is a personal thing, can be dangerous and bordering on the smug, Anyone sitting up in an aeroplane and thinking how clever they are, is asking for the gods to flick their wing tip to remind him that he is really trespassing and is only allowed to do so if he realises he is but mortal. Yes, I still get a slight thrill every time I enter the hangar and see my S.E.5a sitting there looking beautiful.

CHAPTER TWELVE
Gibraltar and India

Saying sorry was something I have had a great deal of practice at. It was early Spring 1945, Steve and I having completed two tours of operations with 141 Squadron, as well as time teaching would-be night fighter pilots and navigators at Cranfield and Twinwoods Farm (4 miles North of Bedford), we were given a more exciting job. We were told to go to Melton Mowbray, pick up a Mosquito, fly it to Gibraltar and there work with the Navy. A couple of days after arriving at Melton Mowbray there was a good Mess party at Cranfield, which it would have been a shame to have missed. The train and bus journey to Cranfield presented no problem and the party was well worth going to.

Unfortunately time sped, so that by the time we had returned to the railway station at Bedford, all trains to Melton had ceased. The only train travelling that night ended at Leicester station, with no trains or buses until breakfast time. Railway stations can be very cold and uninviting places in the early hours. Fed up, hung over, hungry, cold and very much in need of getting our heads down for a while, we staggered into MM around midday, only to hear the Tannoy shouting our names throughout the station with a definite request to report to the Flight Office immediately. Apparently, we had been given a brand new aeroplane, just delivered from the Standard Motors factory, which, before it could be accepted, had to perform a consumption test lasting around an hour and a half. No time for lunch, just time to change into battledress, grab helmets and maps, sign the bumph and get out to the aeroplane.

There she was, the most beautiful Mosquito I'd ever seen. Sparklingly new with no squadron markings painted on her side, just the camouflage, serial number and roundels. So far her flying time was just the delivery flight to MM. I scraped my boots before climbing the ladder into the cockpit; I couldn't dirty such a pristine aircraft which was to be mine alone for the next two or three months.

I carefully went through the starting procedure, called for chocks away and taxied to the runway. Throttles steadily wide and she took to the air, as if eager to reach her proper environment. At ten thousand feet we set course for Berwick-upon-Tweed, our first turning point. Setting cruise power, I flew hands-off to see if any trim would be necessary; just a touch of aileron trim to keep the left wing up, and a little rudder trim to stop her wandering, then she flew beautifully. Layers of cloud prevented us seeing the ground, although just occasionally we caught a glimpse of green below.

My keeping on track was a bit erratic, as I kept dropping off to sleep, then waking with a start, to find the wings at an odd angle. I think Steve was dozing as well, because he had said nothing about the antics of the machine. The further North we flew, the better the weather became and by the time we reached Berwick-upon-Tweed, the cloud had cleared and we had no trouble recognising the bridges over the Tweed.

I knew Berwick from the air, because it was one of the landmarks we used whilst I was at the Operational Training Unit at Charterhall, and I also remembered with some shame an incident concerning those bridges. During our tours of operations with 141 Squadron, Steve and I were conducting high-level interceptions of enemy fighters over France and Germany, trying to protect our bombers from attack. It was also thought that a time might come, especially around D-Day, when we could well be expected to engage in low-level attacks, mainly on trains. To that end, whenever the chance arose we would carry out practice attacks. On the night in question I had been flying my Mosquito in the Berwick-upon-Tweed area, it was a bright, moon-lit night and I had seen the smoke of a locomotive approaching Berwick bridge. Without too much thought I peeled off into a steep dive. The train by then was puffing its way across the bridge giving me a wonderful chance to make a practice attack.

The speed of the Mosquito in the headlong dive increased alarmingly while I was trying to look through the gun sight to bring the locomotive into line and I was so fascinated watching the smoke appearing to zoom up towards me I left the pull-out a bit late. When I realised how close I was, I was far too low to be safe and had to pull hard on the stick to miss the train. The poor engine driver must have had an even bigger fright than I had, I wished I had been able to say sorry to him. I'll bet he told the story a few times.

Back to the consumption test. We were briefed to fly to Berwick upon Tweed, then set a predetermined course out over the North Sea to a specified point, turn and make landfall at Aberdeen. Still tired and still nodding off, the next two legs seemed to take an age but eventually land came into sight. Somehow Aberdeen looked rather odd, and when we got much closer we realised it was not Aberdeen, we were back over Berwick upon Tweed. Either sleepiness or the Mosquito's desire to go home had completely messed up the whole process.

Back at Melton Mowbray it was considered that the amount of petrol used for the time taken was sufficient to pronounce the test successful.

Next day were amused and somewhat annoyed to find we were to be briefed by some upstart how to fly safely to Portreath in Cornwall, including being careful to fly at a safe height around Okehampton, because the nearby hills of Dartmoor are quite high, and to watch the weather as we might encounter clouds at various heights. On and on he droned; I felt like telling him that we had, in the past few months, flown to most of the cities of Europe in conditions which were far from safe and had somehow survived.

The actual flight to Portreath was pretty uneventful. We did try to fly the Mosquito down Cheddar Gorge, but found it impossible to turn in such a tight valley. We did make a little call at Steve's parents' home a few miles from Camelford. Steve's mum came charging out into the back garden waving a tablecloth – why a tablecloth we could never figure out, she said it was 'just in case we couldn't see her'. She had been doing the same caper each of the many times we had beaten the place up.

So to Portreath, to wait for the morrow and the long trip to Gibraltar. The morrow dawned with dove-grey mist, which started to break up when the first streaks of weak sunshine broke through. Steve's job was to obtain a met forecast, the wind conditions and anything concerning what weather we might come across, so he could work out the compass course to allow us to fly out to the

Bishop's Rock lighthouse on the Isles of Scilly, then down the 7° meridian. The Met man had given us a fairly strong westerly wind to contend with, and Steve had made his flight plan accordingly. It was around 9am before the wheels left British soil, and by then the visibility was endless.

We headed out over the last of the mainland and on towards the Isles of Scilly. We knew all this area well from our time when we first joined the Squadron at Predannack on Lizard Point. We passed Bishop's Rock, standing defiant against the Atlantic, and did a final check on all the instruments. All pressures and temperatures correct, the engines running perfectly, driving the massive propellers and giving us a cruise speed just below three hundred miles per hour. What could be better? A beautiful clear morning, sunshine, a placid sea and the excitement of flying to places we had not seen before. Below us four small coasters plodded their way through the calm sea, the smoke from their funnels going straight up. Turn left onto course, next stop Gibraltar.

Doug's Mosquito over the sea near Gibraltar

Having nothing to look at except the sea gets extremely boring, nothing but sea, sea and more sea, sticking to the course Steve had set, and waiting for the first signs of land after we had crossed the Bay of Biscay. Steve, as bored as I was, tried to pick up the BBC Home Service on the radio, but failed. Still we went on and on, until it dawned on me that some kind of land should have come into view. It also dawned on me, the smoke from the coasters had gone straight up; the wind could not have been anything like as strong as the met report had estimated. Consequently, as we had set course a few degrees west of our track to allow for the wind, we were now further out into the Atlantic than we should have been. With no landmarks and no other means of navigation, I had to change course to correct our silly mistake. After a quick mental calculation, I considered that at our present rate we would be unlikely to reach Gibraltar at all if we kept to our flight plan which expected us to take an over-sea route and approach Gibraltar after flying around Trafalgar Point and through the Straits. To hell with General Franco's neutrality, we had to head for Spain and fly a direct route overland.

After turning several degrees to the left on my compass, we eventually sighted land. I reasoned that in case any Spanish gun or plane would try to intercept me, I would fly at 500 feet, low enough to be passed before they woke up and took action. How pleased I was when we crossed the coast and flew a course that I thought would bring us close to our destination.

The land below us was not very exciting, dull brown and uninteresting. We did flash over one Spanish Airforce aerodrome, but all the planes were on the ground and looked as if they had been there since the Civil War in 1936. Probably everyone was at an early siesta. The terrain started to become hilly, with no tarmac roads, only gravel tracks devoid of traffic. Eventually, we got close enough to call Gibraltar Radio on the radio. They came through loud and clear, and we asked for a course to steer for the Rock. They were somewhat taken aback when they gave us a fix and a course to steer. We were supposed to call from Europa Point on the South of the Rock but here we were arriving overland from the north.

With about twenty miles to run, I felt sure I would see Gibraltar sticking out like a sore thumb, but the country was quite hilly, so we couldn't see it until we were very much nearer. We circled in Algeciras Bay, waiting for the main (and only) road between Spain and Gibraltar, which crossed the runway, to be closed to traffic, and then approached to land.

Road across the runway at Gibraltar

Gibraltar is a place where aeroplanes would be the last things anyone would expect to find. The runway at Gib. sticks out into the sea at the western end, crosses the narrow isthmus which joins the towering rock to Spain and ends at the sea-shore on the other side. At the Eastern end is a plaque stating that near here Wladislaw Sikorski, the Polish Prime Minister in exile, was drowned when his Liberator aircraft failed to get airborne. Many strange rumours have, and still do, leave doubts as to why this disaster happened.

Gibraltar held many hazards for the unsuspecting pilot. This great lump of rock sticking up like a wall into the elements has a strange effect on the winds. As the wind hits the rock and rises, it causes water vapour to condense and form cloud, and in certain conditions it can descend and drape the runway in fog. From a different direction, the wind might curl over the rock, causing turbulence which gives anyone trying to land a very bumpy ride. To say the least, it can be great fun.

After we landed, we were directed to the North Front Naval Establishment, where we parked our aeroplane next to a Swordfish and a Beaufighter Mark 2, both of which I thought were obsolete aircraft. Although I'm sure Mosquitos had landed there in the past, an enormous amount of interest was shown by the Naval chaps, who crawled all over it and asked for rides in our machine. Later on, some of these sailors were taken up on legitimate occasions.

Soon after our arrival we were requested to appear before the ground controllers to explain why we had flown over neutral Spain. It was considered by most to be a bit of a joke, but the usual apology was sent to Madrid or wherever. General Franco had, by now, realised that the English were going to win the war, so he dropped his close alliance with Germany, calculating which side his bread was buttered. He had been extremely anti-British when it looked as if success was on Germany's side and even though his attitude changed, he could still hardly be called friendly.

Friendly, however, very much applied to the inhabitants of the Naval Officer's Mess (I believe the correct name for such an establishment is the 'Wardroom'). A handshake was never considered enough of a greeting unless it was accompanied by a pink gin at any time of the day.

Next day we had to apologise to the top man in our own RAF at Gib. He, I believe, spotted a Mosquito on his aerodrome and was annoyed because we had not announced our arrival to him.

We joined the Navy at their base at North Front and didn't have to apologise to anyone for several days. The Navy's Fleet Air Arm contingent at Gib. consisted of a few pilots and fewer aeroplanes. The inmates of the wardroom could not have been more hospitable. The food was good, the bar flowing.

We were conducted around and shown all the sights of Gibraltar. The whole place was a delight. The idea in Gib was, I believe, to convince the Spaniards that everything British was on the up and up. No rationing, no shortages, no war-time austerity. We had the time of our lives. Things we hadn't seen in the shops were there. I bought a sports jacket and some DAKS (trousers from the menswear shop of that name), had a new uniform suit made to measure, bought shoes and shirts all without coupons and very cheap. The civvies were for wearing when crossing the border into Spain, which we did on odd occasions. Very odd.

La Linea, the little town across the border, had the usual collection of small shops, many eating and drinking houses and hundreds of brothels. We shopped, ate and drank and kept well away from the ladies of the night, or in their case, morning, afternoon or any other time. The Spanish army doing their version of the changing of the guards was fun to watch. We were advised only to watch and never laugh. They couldn't stand criticism of any sort. The guards had obviously been hand-picked to show what great variety existed in stature in the Spanish nation. None were the same height, some about five feet one inch, others reaching to at least six foot. Unfortunately for them all, the uniforms were made for the tallest; if that was not quite true, at least all the uniforms had got terribly mixed up and the soldiers had thrown on anything which was to hand. By far the worst garments were the overcoats. The shortest men not only marched, but swept the streets at the same time.

The ship we were to work with eventually arrived. We were taken on board, given a few pink gins by the Commander, then given an outline of the radar tests which they would like to carry out and how we could help them. Before leaving, we were wined and dined, as only destroyer wardrooms can do. Next day we had to apologise to the Governor of Gibraltar for being out after curfew and making a lot of noise.

H.M.S. *Barfleur* was a beautiful sight when we first approached her from the air. She was long, sleek, grey and very, very business-like. Her four guns in two turrets at the sharp end made her look more like the size of a cruiser; going flat out at a great rate of knots she almost disappeared in her own spray. That was how we saw her first. We established contact over the radio. To show off, we stopped one engine, feathered the prop, then proceeded to 'beat up' the ship, coming in very fast from all angles. A voice from the water thanked us for the display, but wondered if we knew that one of our engines had stopped working. Days later, after we had explained some of the workings of aircraft, they caught on, and when next we showed them the one-engined performance, challenged us to stop the other one as well. Each day the ship would send in the programme of trials and we would comply if possible, sometimes spending three-hour stretches at wave-top height in low level mock torpedo runs, until the windscreen became opaque with salt spray. Some days were spent at thirty thousand feet in high-level bombing runs, and being able to look down great stretches of the North African coast for miles, and sometimes dive-bombing the ship and looking straight down the funnel.

HMS *Barfleur*

It was not expected that anything would go radically wrong with the Mozzie during its time at Gib., but it was not long before a minor snag asserted itself. An oil seal on one of the propellers leaked. The only replacements close at hand were at the American Air Force base at Casablanca. Very early one Sunday morning I took the Navy's engineer officer with me and flew down to Casablanca to cadge one from the Yanks. On seeing a Mosquito, I suppose for the first time, the American in the control tower bellowed over the radio with excitement, "Gee, a Sunday morning buzz job, does it go?" I was not quite sure what he meant. As we were still at about fifteen hundred feet, I opened to full throttle and brought the Mozzie down to the ground level and scampered across his field at a great rate, pulling up between the big D.C.4 transport planes parked on the tarmac. His voice, shaking with emotion, pleaded for no more or we'd all be in trouble. After we had landed and parked alongside the D.C.4s, he arrived with many admirers to see this 'limey' missile. We got our oil seal, no trouble. We flew, joyously, back at nought feet along the rocky coast of Morocco, looking up at the Arabs riding their camels along the cliff paths.

The Navy, even after the loss of the *Prince of Wales* and *Repulse* by Japanese aircraft, and the many losses in Norway by German aircraft, still would not realise their vulnerability from the skies. Thinking back to the Falklands Campaign, I still don't think they realise it yet. H.M.S. Barfleur was convinced she could protect herself and when our attacks regularly got through, put it down to lack of practice. They then thought they would like to fire at us using real ammunition. They would, they said, off-set their guns so that they would miss by a prescribed amount, taking a read-off through a graticule to show they were on target. Having sat way up above when they were doing a shoot, and watched one shell explode about ten yards in front of their bows, and the next was so far away it was never seen again, we refused their offer. They didn't really mind, but thought their own fliers would have done it and maybe we were a bit windy.

Occasionally, the ship stayed tied up against the detached mole and we were given the day off. On one such day, I persuaded the Naval C.O. at North Front to let me fly his Seafire and he in return could borrow my Mozzie. I felt I might never have the chance to fly any kind of Spitfire if I was not quick about it. He readily agreed and showed me over the cockpit, pointing out the controls and telling me the dos and don'ts. I was amazed at the lack of forward visibility as I taxied to the runway's end. Weaving from side to side was essential to keep a view of the way ahead and, not being the tallest of people, I had to stand up from time to time to see where I was going. I remembered that poor chap at Predannack who had taxied into me and felt some sympathy. Turning to face the long bit of runway in front of me, I thought of the bronze plaque let into the concrete at the far end. It commemorated the death of the Polish Prime Minister whose Liberator crashed into the sea on take-off earlier in the war. I opened the throttle, waited for the tail to rise so that I could see the end of the runway approaching, gently eased back on the control column and was a couple of hundred feet above the plaque by the time I'd got there.

Seafire at Gibraltar

The 'chassis', or undercarriage, of the Spitfire needs careful handling, otherwise if activated ham-handedly or too quickly, it could jam. I took my time. She climbed steadily, I levelled off at two thousand feet and flew around just to the east of the rock. This Seafire was very responsive, although not as fast as I had hoped. I threw it around a bit, pressing myself down into the seat with the positive 'G' force. I enjoyed myself for an hour, trying out stalls, tight turns and various gyrations. I was impressed with this thoroughbred. I still felt a little uneasy about flying over the sea with only one engine, having been spoilt with my Mosquito, so I returned to the rock. I knew the approach and landing would be very different from my Mozzie. For one thing, the forward visibility vanished when the undercarriage and flaps were lowered and the nose came into the approach attitude. The only way was the curving swoop with the nose to one side and me looking diagonally at the runway. It worked. The wheels touched, swayed and stayed down. I had flown a Spitfire, or the Navy's equivalent, and was very proud.

Seeing I had swapped two engines for one, I felt I deserved another aircraft to make up for it and, seeing that they had another single-engined aircraft going begging, I plumped for that. It was a Swordfish. There it stood, the ultimate in Christmas trees, all struts and wires and looking like a thing from the past. I collected the ground crew and started the climb to the cockpit. Up and up, hand over hand, reaching for the cockpit coaming and eventually dragging legs over and settling into the vast seat. By the time I was strapped in, the mechanics were sweating and heaving on the great handle which wound up the starter flywheel. Their usual comments, between gasps for air, were to the effect that 'if the engine does not start first time, the pilot gets out to turn the handle'. Praise be, it started first time, so all was well. The radial engine made a remarkably reluctant clatter as it chuntered into life, smoking and belching, till settling down into a more organised rattle. I was cast off and steered towards mid-runway.

The take-off was astounding. I have always loved the story of how Bellerophon had captured Pegasus, the winged horse, by leaping on to its back, placing the bridle round its head and flying off into the blue. I was the modern-day Bellerophon, only my mount was a cart horse. We swayed along, first one wheel leaving the ground, then the other, by then the first had grounded again and we were still trying to get unstuck. All of a sudden the gavotte stopped and we ballooned into the air. Before take-off, I had asked for the various speeds required to fly in various situations and was told, "Climb at sixty, cruise at sixty, land at sixty." After that I didn't bother to look at the speed, it seemed to know what to do. I spent another wonderful hour waltzing around the Med. My flight was in warm and clear weather. How, I wondered, did anyone fly these things from heaving carrier decks in bitter conditions and then try to fight? How could anyone at the 'top' send pilots on missions in these things? My opinion of naval thinking plunged.

My only experience of trying to manage a Corsair was at Gibraltar when I volunteered to taxi such a creature from one end of the North Front to the other. I decided there and then never to fly it! American aeroplanes, like typical American airmen, were big. The average Yank had arms modelled on the gorilla, which gave him the ability to stretch to the extremes of the American aircraft's cockpit. Cockpit drill must have been horrendous when most of the switches were placed in rows on a panel all looking exactly the same. How anyone flew at night is anybody's guess.

Corsair at Gibraltar

We had only been at Gib. for a day or two when we were joined by a second Mosquito and crew. This crew, like us, had finished a couple of tours of Ops and were now being what was called 'rested'. The four of us were invited to spend a weekend aboard a small aircraft carrier from which the Corsair had flown. The method to 'come aboard' was to travel out into the bay on a 'lighter' which carried a Corsair on its platform of a deck. When alongside the ship, some loud ringing voice from the flight deck many feet above shouted, "You there," (meaning me) "Bend the line on her." I assume he meant 'tie the rope', which dangled above me, onto the aeroplane. Phraseology differs from one service to another; to 'bend' anything in the RAF, especially aeroplanes, means to cause some damage to them.

Knowing this I stood there looking stupid, which was not appreciated by the shouting Chief Petty Officer above. I'm sure that if I had obliged by tying the hoist rope onto this aeroplane it would have slipped its knot and descended with a bang on my head. Fortunately, some sailor chap appeared and 'bent the rope' in true Naval fashion and up the Corsair went to its home on the deck above. The carrier itself was one of the smaller variety, called by Fleet Air Arm a 'Woolworth Carrier', whether because of the cost or the size I know not. The flight deck was correspondingly short, rather like comparing a full-size tennis court to a table-tennis table. No wonder planes kept charging into the barrier net and, in RAF parlance, 'bending' something. After a very instructive and alcoholic weekend I was so glad I had my Mosquito waiting for me.

Another experience happened on yet another day off of quite a different nature. Steve had dashed off to the beach with one of the very few W.R.E.N.S. on the Rock and I was at North Front, when a request arrived asking for an air-sea-rescue flight. I told the controller of my lack of a navigator, but he said he could direct me from base and through the radio of another aircraft flying high. Would I fly low and take my cue from him?

Off I went, being directed through the straits, past Cape Trafalgar and up the Spanish coast. Flying at below one thousand feet, I was to look for a Liberator, which might have crashed anywhere along the line I was to take. I flew for ages, occasionally talking to the aircraft above. Neither of us had seen anything resembling a crash. Eventually, with the afternoon wearing on, we were told to return to base.

I nosed in towards the coast to where the low sun lit up the sandstone cliffs. By now I had decided that, as the search was over, I could please myself at what height I would fly home. Following the coast at about two hundred feet above the water was marvellous. The cliffs, all burnt sienna, yellow ochre and crimson were an inspiring sight. Suddenly an inlet appeared, opening into a harbour. In I flew to find what looked like a town of the Middle Ages grouped around the waterfront. It was quite beautiful. I made one circuit then flew out again through the gap, not feeling I should trespass into such an ancient place with such a new contraption as an aeroplane. Francis Drake didn't care quite so much when he had sailed into Cadiz harbour almost four hundred years before.

Wreckage was found of the Liberator some days later, but it was many miles from where we had been searching.

Our stay at Gibraltar came to an end, but not before we had been, on Easter Sunday, to a bullfight in La Linea. We went with a small gang of sailors, one of whom had to rush out to be sick when he saw all the blood. The local spectators didn't like us much when we cheered the bull and not the matador. Then the real end came with a party on board the ship. I'm glad I cannot remember what went on. The first half-hour was reasonable enough, but some great Lieutenant Commander kept thrusting pint glasses at me full of almost colourless liquid, and I, being stupid, drank them. The next day, at one thousand feet, looking through a thick alcoholic haze, we followed the ship through the straits wishing her Bon Voyage and apologising profusely for anything awful we might have done the previous evening.

After another twenty-four hours to recover, we loaded the Mozzie with bananas and a few pairs of silk stockings and headed back to England. The customs officer who met us at Portreath had motored from Falmouth to collect the equivalent of eight pence, the duty on the stockings. It could hardly have been worth it.

After breakfast the following day, we took off for Melton Mowbray, circling Steve's home at Camelford on the way, to let his people know we had arrived back. The man at Melton Mowbray was furious. "We send aircraft out, we do not expect them to come back, we have no provision for accepting aircraft, only dispatching them," he growled. On and on he droned. For a fleeting moment, I thought of leaping back into my beautiful Mosquito and flying away to somewhere where it would be mine forever, and away from the horrors of those who thought of aeroplanes as just things to be sent hither and thither. I didn't. In a way, I wish I had. In the end Steve and I listened to no more moans, plonked the paper-work on this hero's desk, indicated, with a gesture, that victory was close, and left to go, by train, to OTU.

A short stay at Cranfield and then embarkation leave. During leave, the war in Europe was wound up and V.E. day was to be celebrated on the day of my return. My celebrations were dashed when, on returning to Cranfield, I had a letter waiting for me, telling me that my old school-friend Jim was dead. I had seen him only once since Rhodesian days when I'd flown up to Binbrook in a Beau. He was a gunnery leader on a Lancaster bomber squadron, which meant he was not only in charge of a squadron-load of gunners, but had to fill in if any crew was incomplete. He had done just that for a raid on Augsburg and never returned. I wrote back to his Irish nurse, whom he'd only recently married. It was impossible to put into words how I felt. I imagine my efforts were most inadequate. On V.E. night there was dancing in the streets. I tried to join in on the streets of Woburn Sands but my heart wasn't in it. I left the celebrations early and cycled back to Cranfield alone.

A lesser tragedy occurred during that leave. Some bright spark had been through my belongings, stored in my room, and stolen, apart from other things, my Smith and Wesson revolver. I was wrong to have left it there. I tried hard to report the loss to various armament officers, but the reply was always the same, "Please don't tell me, it'll cause such a fuss." The best thing, I was told, was to go wherever I was going and bother someone else. I stuffed the holster with the Daily Mirror and proceeded, once again to Glasgow to catch the boat to India.

My first voyage by troopship to Durban in 1941 was to be likened to the old slave traffic. Hundreds and hundreds of us crammed below decks with no room to move. The whole floor was covered with mess tables and benches set athwartships and screwed to the floor. Eighteen of us, nine each side with just enough elbow room to use a knife and fork. Above, hanging from the ceiling, were hooks for hammocks, and above them, storage racks for kit bags, and that was home for six weeks. There were no portholes, we were on the waterline. When boat drill was ordered, it would take twenty minutes to get everyone up and on deck. As we were resident on the bottom shelf, we were always last to reach the fresh air. If boat drill had been for real, I think my chances of survival would have been nil. I was told we had over five thousand souls aboard. And I couldn't swim. After that trip I learned to swim in the warm, African waters in readiness for the home journey.

The old *Moultan* was, for us, a hell ship. The food was disgusting and almost everything else was slightly below that standard. I envied the officers with their cabins on the upper decks, living the life of the upper classes.

In 1945 my transport to India was aboard the *Highland Chieftain*. Before becoming a troopship, she carried meat from one end of the world to the other in refrigerated holds. The lads living below had beautifully cool quarters and mess decks, while we snobs were stuck up on deck level in appalling heat, especially in the Red Sea. The three weeks of boredom on the ship was broken only by the day parked at Port Said and the sights along the Suez Canal. Eventually, Bombay, with, like the rest of India, the incredible contrasts. Opulence on the one hand, like the Taj Mahal Hotel with its air conditioning and comfort, and the gutter dwellers, poor and disabled beggars, on the other. India was obviously going to be a country to marvel at, but not necessarily like. We could only accept what we found, without being able to do anything about it.

After suffering a hot and dusty train journey, I arrived at an RAF Maintenance Unit at Allahabad. The purpose, I was told in England, was to go there to join a team of test pilots testing Mosquitoes, whose health was becoming impaired by the climatic conditions and to see if the improvements the experts had incorporated into the strength of the machines were working. So far, a number of pilots had had the tails of their Mozzies break off after the planes had suffered the extremes of the Indian weather. They, the unfortunates, failed to recover from the resultant dives and so gave little information of what and how things had happened. At this M.U. a variety of aircraft were constantly passing through, some for repair, some for inspection and maintenance, some to be un-crated and put together, and even some to be written off.

The two flights, A and B, were situated at almost opposite sides of the aerodrome, A flight dealing with all the single engined aircraft and B flight the twin-engined variety. We tried to do all the test flying before lunch, which meant starting pretty early in the morning. As the day wore on, the turbulent conditions became worse, as the earth became hotter and hotter, so that by lunch-time flying was bumpy and difficult. Anyone working on the aeroplanes on the ground found them impossibly hot to get into.

The monsoon weather presented another hazard. The torrential rain would cool the atmosphere for a while, making life a little easier, until the humidity started to play hell with man and machine. Wooden Mosquitoes split their spars, when some glues came unstuck, Beaus suffered some electrical troubles and, all in all, we would have been better off if they had been fitted with floats. All men from the M.O. to the A.C.2s suffered from 'prickly heat', which brought with it a measles-like rash and intolerable itching. After the morning break for 'tea and wads' (tea and buns), the whole flight to a man would stand, legs astride, shirts unbuttoned, arms held away from bodies and suffer, with the great desire to scratch and tear at the torment, and all the time, with great will-power, refraining from doing so in the knowledge that it would only make things worse.

Beaufighters and Mosquitoes were to be my main occupation. Life was interesting and sometimes exciting. Diving the Mozzie to four hundred and fifty miles per hour, then pulling out fairly smartly, was part of the test; I suppose to see if the tail would stay on. Fortunately, the ones I flew did. In test-work one expects things to go wrong and one is often not to be disappointed. I had

Mozzies shed spinners, lose fabric from ailerons, burst tyres, give insufficient engine revs, over-rev, suffer hydraulic trouble, suffer electrical trouble, shed oil, get the shakes and go bang, and on one momentous occasion after an almighty bang, lose the blades from some part of the supercharger. Then the other engine started playing up. Sounding like a bag of nails was an apt description of the noise which accompanied me down to a one-engined landing - really a half-engine landing.

Single-engined landings became all the rage, when a boost capsule burst after takeoff, or when a propeller feathered and would not un-feather, or when an oil pressure became uncommonly low. One heavily-laden Beaufighter Mark 10, equipped with its two-hundred gallon tank, like a torpedo, underneath, also rocket rails under the wings and various radar bumps on top of the fuselage, decided that one engine should have been enough to take off with, so promptly banged and clattered and stopped its starboard Hercules just after I had got the wheels up. I managed three-quarters of a circuit before it fell out of the air just within the aerodrome boundary, but missed the runway in use. I had just got the wheels down at the last minute. The Beau bounded to a halt, being followed by the fire engine and ambulance, who were fast to respond and were annoyed to find they had no custom. The chief at the hangar said, "It must have been inhibiting oil left on the plugs." I suppose I should have been annoyed. All manner of other incidents cropped up, keeping all of us on our toes; still, it was fun and there were other compensations.

When work was slack in my flight, I would wander over to the other side and fly their Spitfires and Hurricanes. I had flown the Seafire at Gibraltar, now the real Spitfires. It was a nice change to fly single-engined aircraft occasionally. One blessing was being able to take-off and land with the canopy open to allow a cooling draught to flow in. The firing range for the testing of the aircraft's guns was a patch of river-bank a few miles down the Ganges from Allahabad, marked out by several white-painted, forty-gallon drums. To check harmonisation and fireability we would fly to the range, dive onto the target and open fire. As soon as the guns started to rattle, small Indian lads would appear from the bushes to collect the spent brass cartridge cases which fell from the aircraft. Eventually, this brass would probably turn up in the bazaars as Benares brass plates and vases. I tested one Spitfire at the firing range, when only one gun, the cannon on the port side, decided to fire. The Spit slewed violently, spraying shells well away from the target. I hoped none of the brass collectors were about.

Some Austers, light spotter planes, were delivered to the M.U. in boxes. These, when assembled, were tested. One of the tests was an hour's consumption flight. Their glass-house perspex cabins attracted all the heat going. I ended up, after the hour, like an over-ripe and very dehydrated tomato.

The last word in Spitfires arrived - the Spitfire Mark XIV. They were very different from the lesser marks; their Griffon engines were so much bigger and more powerful. The engine bearer was totally redesigned to hold the enormous power plant. The fuselage had to be strengthened, the rudder reshaped, and all manner of modifications to make this one of the fastest aeroplanes about. Some of the XIVs had teardrop canopies, making the all-round visibility very good indeed. Some had five-bladed propellers. All had an overwhelming desire to charge off down the runway at an angle of forty-five degrees from their original direction. Once airborne, they would stick their noses in the air and climb like nothing I had ever experienced. Modern jet pilots probably think nothing of tremendous rates of climb, but for us oldies the Spitfire XIV was fantastic. It also had a tendency to vibrate, enough at times to shake your teeth out.

The Hurricane was quite different: slow, sedate, kindly, steady and with quite an 'old aeroplane' feel about it. On first meeting, I wondered how the pilots of the Battle of Britain could possibly fight in such a staid old aeroplane. After I had got used to them, I found out. They could turn on a sixpence, take all the 'G' force that you could put on to them, and still remain a wonderfully steady gun platform when required to be. I began to like them.

Extra jobs cropped up on occasions. Once I delivered a Beaufighter to a remote spot in Burma, left it there, and returned with a Mozzie which needed repair. I couldn't think why the tree-lined strip was deserted when I'd arrived. I learned that some 'big cat', of what species I never found out, had been patrolling around that morning and the inhabitants were taking no chances. I was quite happy to cut my visit short and be on my way.

Another occasion took me on a prolonged chase for spares of some sort, nearly completely round India. Starting from Allahabad, first stop Calcutta, then Cuttack for the first night. On next day to Madras, Trichinopoly and across to Cochin. I stayed a day or two there with the Navy who had a Fleet Air Arm station there. Home again took me to Bangalore, Hyderabad, Nagpur, thence to Allahabad. It was a wonderful sight-seeing trip, which I would have enjoyed a lot more if a few more things had been in my favour. The weather was mid-monsoon with thunder-clouds chasing me all the way round. The Beau complained the whole way, rattling and banging and needing a pep talk and new plugs at Cochin. The rear cupola broke from its hinges and smashed. Oil spewed from every pore. It was scrapped as soon as we got back. I say, we, because I had taken a Navigator with me. He was an architect in Civvy Street. He loved the sights, but hated the Beau.

On a nicer occasion, a nice quiet Sunday, I flew a Mozzie to Delhi. This plane had been stripped of its guns and ammunition, and had racks fitted to take Sir Basil Embry's cases and luggage. He was to fly, in a hurry, to England. On the way to Delhi, I diverted from the direct route, to fly to Agra and inspect the Taj Mahal. It is best seen by moonlight, so I've been told. Circling it at eight hundred feet on a Sunday morning can be recommended for a super view.

Sir Basil was waiting impatiently on the tarmac at Palam, the Delhi airport, surrounded by masses of top brass. Haste was the top priority. I was dragged out and replaced by Sir B. and his flapping navigator. The engines were started and off went the Mozzie like a shot, to the take-off point. It was a pity Sir B. had forgotten to open the radiator shutters. The engines boiled on the way to the holding point and issued clouds of steaming glycol all over the place. Everything had to stop for a cooling-off period. He got away eventually and took off like a frightened kangaroo. I think he must have been out of practice, or didn't realise how light the stripped-down Mozzie was.

The chief test pilot at Delhi found me another interesting job. I was to take over the little test flight at Lahore. The real reason for going to Lahore was to co-operate with Professor F.S. Gill, a learned Indian, who, after spending years in America researching the antics of cosmic rays, had returned to continue his work in his own country. This necessitated loading his equipment into a bomber-type Mosquito and flying it up to great heights, while the learned Prof. counted from his apparatus, the hard particles, or mesons or whatever they are called these days, as they sped earthwards through the atmosphere. Many and various theories were forwarded as to the advantages of knowing what cosmic rays were all about, everything from weather forecasting to atomic power. All of this left me baffled. I was only there to do the flying. The Air Commodore at Delhi, who met the Prof. and me, seemed to think it worthwhile. The Mozzie was fitted up with various gadgets, mostly argon tubes suspended in gimbals in the Mozzie's nose. Wire trailed around all over the place, with the Prof. swearing away in a Chicago accent every time some of his uninsulated wires gave him a shock.

Eventually, with all the instruments installed, we flew a number of high flights above the vicinity of Lahore. At thirty-five thousand feet up, the line of snow-covered Himalayan mountains was easily visible. They looked most spectacular and I would have loved to have gone a lot closer. I did try, later on, but still did not get as close as I would have liked. That expedition was on foot, and not in the air.

The next series of experiments with the Prof. were to take place around the magnetic equator, which, I was told, lay just to the south of Ceylon. All arrangements were made to fly to the island. Unfortunately, the Mozzie developed glue trouble, the very thing we all dreaded might happen to wooden aircraft in the tropics. The main spar laminations started to come unstuck. No other aeroplane could be made available, so the experiments came to a halt.

Doug with ground crew and Professor Gill at Lahore

I returned to Allahabad for a week or two, and by the time I took up my Lahore test flight again, the cosmic ray venture was a thing of the past. During my stay at Lahore, various odd aeroplanes needed testing. A Dakota or two arrived. They looked pretty big and I felt needed two people to fly them if life was to be comfortable. Actually, I found difficulty reaching back to the undercarriage lever.

My living accommodation was a shared bungalow, for the four of us; the Station Administration Officer, the Doctor, the Dentist and me. One of the others, usually the Dentist, found time to down tools, and become my second pilot. We had a pact - he wouldn't hurt me when I was in his chair, if I didn't frighten him when he was in my aeroplane. The partnership was very successful, especially in the Dakota. I thought the Dak a splendid bus; big, docile, good on one engine and generally easy to fly. I can see why there are quite a few still working for their living even now.

The end of the war in Japan, although ending with a bang, had come and gone during the time that I was in Allahabad. The celebrations were nothing to write home about. The government, under Mr Attlee, had made many promises, especially to do with the demobilization of thousands in the forces. The forgotten services of East Asia still felt forgotten. News from home gave the impression that all the good jobs were being snapped up by the people on the spot. Discontented agitators demonstrated all over the place and life became tedious. All this, coupled with much worse agitation from the Indians, who had been promised 'Home Rule', and were intent on rather un-peaceful carryings-on to hurry it up, gave most of us the urge to leave them and their country to sort it out for themselves. I felt sorry for an awful lot of Indians, Anglo-Indians and the like, who dreaded the departure of the British, with good reason - the Indians, because so many would lose their jobs; the Anglo-Indians because they might lose their lives.

Flying still continued. Aeroplanes still needed repairing and testing, although the old-timers of the peacetime Airforce had already painted white lines along the floor of the hangars up to which the wheels of their aeroplanes were to be placed and if possible, never moved.

An untidy and sand-encrusted Spitfire had been cluttering up the tarmac ever since I had been there and was now to be got rid of. It was wheeled into the hangar, worked on for ages and brought back to flyable serviceability. I tested it, when it was ready, and by sheer over-confidence nearly killed myself in the process. It flew quite well. To show how well, I whistled into a slow roll, at about twelve hundred feet above the control tower, for all to see. I had lost a little height but decided on another roll. Over and onto the upside-down position; I felt a decided lack of speed, then a decided lack of anything else in the way of control. The nose fell. I was diving straight down towards a long row of sheds, which appeared to be coming up much too fast. Easing the stick back as much as possible without flicking out, I could feel the Spit only just responding. I missed the sheds, not by a lot but enough to frighten me into a very mortified state.

When I landed, my fitter was full of enthusiasm for the daring display. I crept away quietly.

One morning, a most odd contraption was wheeled out for me to test. It was a Vultee Vengeance, a great barrel of an aircraft. Designed as a dive bomber, this great single-engined beast looked as if it had been thought up by the builders of battleships.

Doug beside a Vultee Vengeance

I clambered up to the cockpit, using the several hand-and-foot holds, slid back the canopy and stepped in. There was enough room to swing several cats, and that was only my bit. Behind the long greenhouse hood was another position, way back, for an air-gunner. I believe, originally, this aircraft was the American version of the German Stuka dive-bomber. It never caught on in Europe, hence its appearance in the Far East, as far away as possible. This was the first one I had ever seen. I spent some minutes fathoming out all the bits and knobs and, as usual in American aeroplanes, finding I was not big enough to reach them all. During the taxi out, I felt very much like the time I drove a traction engine, having a great boiler in front but very little control over it. It needed its enormous radial engine to get it going. During the test flight I tried to formate on a friendly Dakota, but found it difficult to keep up. When trying the dive brakes, which shot out of the wings like metallic sheep hurdles, the whole craft shook with uncontrollable ague. I was glad to wallop it back onto the runway.

A much more beautiful aeroplane turned up for my attention in the form of a De Havilland Dominie. Some benevolent Maharajah, at the beginning of the war, placed his aeroplanes at the disposal of the RAF. Now that the war was over, the RAF decided to return the compliment by giving him a couple of Dominies. My job, along with the Maharajah's own engineer, was to pass them fit. The engineer was far from fit and was sick on the first test flight. A flight up to Peshawar, on the North West Frontier, was part of the deal, to pick up some bits and pieces. The mountainous terrain over which I flew, low level of course, was most spectacular and exciting. One whole stretch of jagged peaks reminded me of bluey-grey sharks' teeth, ready to snap at any moment. If any kind of forced landing became necessary, it would have been a difficult job to find a flat enough piece of ground to put down. Looking down, I could imagine hordes of murderous-looking Pathans charging around with their long guns, just waiting for any unsuspecting Britisher to trespass onto their domain. I was glad I had two engines, and both running contentedly. The Dominie was obviously designed by people who knew about piloting, probably A.E. Hagg or Geoffrey De Havilland himself. It had everything to hand and where you wanted it. Sitting way up the front in the narrow pointed nose gave a great feeling of command. Glancing back at the braced wings lent a lovely feeling of old world biplane with the singing wires. All the De Havilland aeroplanes which I have flown have been excellent, and gave the impression of being designed by pilots for pilots.

As the manager of the Test Flight, I could fly just about any plane which turned up. I did draw the line at a Lancaster, which arrived with a revolution counter not working. I ran the engine after a new component had been fitted, but felt it didn't need an air test as everything apart from that was O.K.

Size isn't everything. Sometimes big is better, but not always. When I think back to the Beau and Mossie, I consider they were a fair size for a fighter. At Allahabad I came across some of the American single-seat fighters and considered them to be enormous. Over on the South side of the aerodrome, where I used to go to fly Hurricanes and Spitfires, I saw a great shiny barrel of an aircraft, called by the Yanks the 'Jug'. Its reputation was terrific, fast, agile, and with great endurance. I felt I must have a look, but of course I was too small for it. Trying it for size is all very well but if you are, like me, the wrong size, then things become difficult; when I sat in it I could hardly see above the cockpit sills.

I also read on the instrument panel 'Water Injection'. I had heard of this contraption, but had no idea how to use it, so I decided to leave well alone. I shouldn't have been on that side of the test flight anyway, so I gave up and stayed with the things I knew something about. Speaking to the test pilot who flew the 'Jug', or to give it its proper name, the Thunderbolt, he was not terribly impressed, declaring that it was very good at going downhill. We flew alongside each other the next day, and he found it difficult to keep up with the Mossie at any height.

The Fairchild Argus, a small four-seat, high wing monoplane was to be delivered to Jodhpur by members of Ferry Command. As no-one in our pool of Ferry Command pilots had ever flown one, and as no-one in Ferry Command was allowed to fly anything unless they were current on the type, I asked for and got the job. I think the Argus was the Americans' idea of a small airborne motor car. It had plush roof linings, nicely upholstered seats, ashtrays and arm rests. The distance direct from Lahore to Jodhpur was too great for the little Argus to fly without refuelling, so I flew first to Delhi, then across part of the Thar desert. The trip was full of wondrous sights. The desert was anything but flat. Ridges of hills crossed the track, and on the tops of some of the hills were built fortresses, which looked as if they had been there for thousands of years. The hazy blue-brown barrenness of the desert merged into the dusty sky, making it difficult to distinguish the horizon. I hated to think what it must have been like for the red-coated British soldiers, in the days of the Raj, marching mile after mile in blistering heat. I dismissed the thought and listened to the beat of the single engine.

As we neared our destination, in the late afternoon, silhouetted against the sky, appeared the great dome of the Maharajah's new palace, perched well above the town. Further along, at the end of the ridge, forming an escarpment, and growing up from the sheer cliff face, the great fort stood, defiant against all comers. It was the kind of place that looked as if it had been built for a Hollywood film. I would not have been surprised if Gary Cooper or Errol Flynn were around somewhere. We RAF people had been loaned the Maharajah's old palace for our accommodation. It was close to the old town and boasted the most amazing Victorian-cum-Indian plumbing imaginable. The pipes must have been fitted by a snake charmer, they were so serpentine. Perforated tubes hung above all the windows and poured a constant stream of water down the panes. It kept the place cool, but gave the impression of a perpetual monsoon storm.

I delivered the Argus and returned to Lahore, sitting uncomfortably in the fuselage of a meat-carrying Dakota, which was empty except for smears of blood and bits of fat. It was very cold.

I was still carrying my Daily Mirror revolver. I had often marched boldly through the streets of Calcutta, while the hostile natives were letting us know, in no mean fashion, to 'quit India'. I carried it when visiting the back streets of Allahabad, when some anti-British gents threw house-bricks at me from their vantage point on the top of a two-storey building's flat roof. It looked dramatically protective when the acid throwers were around in Bombay. The stiff upper lip is never quite stiff when the gun, is made of paper as mine was. I only hoped I'd never have to open the holster and threaten a Muslim or Hindu with the writings of Cassandra or the pictures of Jane (both features of the Daily Mirror at that time).

Fortunately for me, there came to live on the station an electrical engineer who had just left Burma, and was, in a roundabout way, making for England and Demob. He had discovered a Smith and Wesson revolver in a deserted jungle clearing and now wondered what to do with it. I think he was quite pleased to get rid of the thing to me. I was pleased to accept, wrote the number onto my accoutrement card, and later handed it into the armoury just before leaving India. I was more than thankful.

Hundreds and hundreds of American aircraft littered the aerodromes of India, mostly Flying Fortresses and Liberators. These planes had been amassing in the Far East as part of the build-up for the crushing of Japan. The atomic bomb had brought about such a swift cessation of hostilities that all these aircraft became redundant almost over-night. Runways were lined with these unwanted craft, all carrying gallons of petrol and sitting in the sun. What happened to them in the end, I hate to think.

The Yanks were only interested in keeping their small communication aircraft, the Beech 18, or Expeditor, as it was named by the RAF. It had twin engines, twin tails and was dual-controlled. The radios were efficient and usually worked quite well. The only snag which I was told to look out for, was a tendency for the undercarriage oleos to stick up, not usually both at once, which would give the aeroplane a very lop-sided look. I tested a few in readiness for their return to American bases in Europe where they were, supposedly, needed.

The Expeditor was another airborne motor-car. The interior was beautifully finished, with leather seats for half a dozen passengers to ride in a fair amount of comfort and good visibility. A great deal of noise was excluded by insulation materials on the insides. The cockpit was quite well designed. The throttle, mixture and other controls all had good-looking mock ivory knobs. The whole machine had an air of plushy opulence, fit for a V.I.P.'s travel. Not an airborne jeep, more an aerial Packard.

By early 1946 I had stored up a whole year's leave with a view to hiking into Tibet, taking six weeks to walk a vast distance and back again over snowy passes and minor mountains. The unrest in the services brought about by the political situation was becoming a right headache. I was not at all interested in my demob, more in my holiday, but I had to give my word before I was allowed to go that, if my demobilisation call came up, I was to return to base immediately, or no doubt questions would be asked as to why I had not been repatriated when I should have been.

Off I went by train, passing some wonderful station names. Apart from a holy ma,n who shared the compartment with two army captains and myself, the trip from Lahore to Calcutta was not too bad. This henna-headed, white-robed pilgrim owned a great deal of property in the best parts of Calcutta and was very rich. It didn't stop him from accepting cheap cigarettes from his followers, who barged into our compartment, for his blessing, at every stop. I got very cross when he would keep spitting on the floor and told him off in my most severe English, backed up with stern gestures. He stopped, but I'm sure understood nothing of what I had actually said.

At Calcutta I stayed one night in the Grand Hotel. Every evening, I was told, a great procession of Indians on bicycles raced around the streets shouting and displaying their 'Quit India' placards. I watched them, on that evening, from the balcony of the hotel. I agreed with their sentiments, but not their riotous insistence. Train again the next day to Siliguri, and then motorcar, and lorry when the car broke down, to Kalimpong.

The sight of the mountain Kanchenjunga, from the hotel's bathroom window, was absolutely stunning. Although it was some miles away, it was spectacular, reaching up and up in dazzling majesty. In the hotel's visitors' book I found the names of George Mallory and Andrew Irvin and other expedition members. They had stayed there on their way to Mount Everest in the nineteen-twenties. George and Andrew were not to return. I was to return - a telegram awaited me demanding it. I had given my word, so back I had to go. By the time I'd reached Lahore, I had spent about ten days continuously train travelling. Now I was to pack up, sign off, and get the train to Bombay and the boat for home. It was May 1946.

Bombay was teeming with exasperated service-men all waiting and waiting. Amongst some who had been there for at least three weeks was my test flight navigator. He was an extremely well-mannered Warrant Officer, who I'm sure would still be there now if I had not found him. Through reading yards of bumph pinned to the notice board, I realised that the very Expeditor Aircraft which I had been testing were waiting at Jodhpur for crews to ferry them to Germany. I insisted, to some chap in charge of things, that we were a willing crew and also insisted that I was flown to Jodhpur, as I'd had enough train travel to last me a life-time. By now, I had picked up a stray wireless operator, who was also Blighty bound. He came from my home town and, although good company, was hopeless as an operator of wireless sets. Throughout the whole journey from Jodhpur to Munich he did not once manage to contact anyone or anything, on his box of tricks.

We took ten days to complete the trip and what a wonderful trip it was. Serviceability was the biggest worry. Nowhere en route could we expect to find any spare parts should anything go wrong. We were ordered to fly in company with another Expeditor, not in formation or anything but leaving and arriving at the same aerodromes along the way. My partner was a very disgruntled chap who felt the RAF had overlooked him when any promotions came along. His aeroplane stayed with us for the first day, then somehow I lost him and never saw him again. The first leg, Jodhpur to Karachi, was quite straightforward. One night in Karachi convinced me that leaving India was a good thing. The natives were not friendly. Karachi to Jiwani, at the tip of what is now Pakistan, was rather a seaside trip along the coast and in beautiful weather with good visibility. It was there that I decided to lose our disgruntled friend by shooting off across the Gulf of Oman before he knew what had happened. Sharjah was the next step, an old RAF base with many and varied stories to tell, of desert madness suffered by the 'bods' who had stayed there too long.

From there to Bahrain. Bahrain Island, sand and more sand with dozens of huts housing German prisoners-of-war, all dreaming of getting home, and not a Nazi amongst them. I am told I would not recognise the place now. I can only remember it as fairly undesirable.

During this part of the trip, we were, and had been, dressed in bush jackets and khaki slacks, so that differences in rank were shown by our hats or chevrons or epaulette ribbons, all of which were take-off-able. On some stations the sergeants' mess was streets better than the officers' - better food, better accommodation and a better time had by all. We all became N.C.O's. If the officers' mess proved to be the best, then we all became officers. Very wicked, I'm sure, but we were going home for demob and couldn't care less. On and on we flew in nice comfortable hops, never more than two and a half hours in length, stopping for meals at meal-times and stopping for the night around tea-time, when the reconnaissance for the best mess would start. On again, and overflying Basra to call at Shaibah, in more desert. It was there in 1941 that the upstart Rashid Ali attempted to make a take-over bid for the RAF station by amassing troops all around. He ended up with a very bloody nose and retreated at great speed. I could quite see why the services' 'lament' of *Shaibah Blues* had such significance.

Eventually, we reached the coast of the Mediterranean, called into Lydda for lunch, then set off for Egypt. The Pyramids could be seen for miles. Slowly Cairo loomed into view. A sprawl of buildings, some magnificent, some squalid. The outskirts of the town looked as if they were trying to push back the desert as far as the pyramids themselves but couldn't quite make it. I made a low circuit around the great monuments, for I knew it would be a long time before I ever saw them again. So far I never have.

Cairo West, the aerodrome, was a blustery, gritty place and I was glad to be off again. Small sand-storms swirled all the way along the Western Desert from El Alamein in Egypt to Cape Bon in Tunisia, giving us no trouble, though I imagine it was fairly uncomfortable on the ground. On over Tobruk, then Benghazi harbour, still full of sunken ships. From then on the whole coastal strip was one long junk yard. Broken tanks and lorries littered the route. Crashed and abandoned aeroplanes of various types and nationalities marked the Eighth Army's progress. One Flying Fortress which had ditched close to a beach looked in perfect condition, apart from being a couple of feet under water, all except the tail which stuck out like a tomb-stone. This desert, a metallic graveyard, reinforced to me the awfulness of wars. We had flown over the whole battlefield; some poor beggars had walked it.

Along the route so far, we had come across a few crews waiting for spare bits to service their Expeditors which had broken down. One Group Captain rushed out to greet us in the hope that we were bringing his replacement tail wheel, which held been waiting three weeks for. He looked very disappointed when he found we had not got it, but carried on waiting. It was good of him not to have demanded our aeroplane and let us wait.

The jump from Tunis to Sardinia was going to be a long one, and a wet one if anything should go wrong. We unearthed our 'Mae West' life jackets from the baggage compartment in the nose of our aircraft, checked our navigation thoroughly and set off for Cagliari on the south side of Sardinia. Lots of sea later, we landed at the island's Italian Air Force base. It still had the odd three-engined sea-plane sitting around on the slip-ways. As in much of North Africa, loads of dazzling white concrete must have been used for almost every building. The officers' mess was the same, and on this occasion, our mutual choice. My balcony overlooked the flag-pole, on which flew the RAF flag, until a party of rather scruffy Italian airmen came to pull it down. I was never sure of the drill for the pulling down of flags, especially if everyone is lumbered with a rifles. This chap had no doubts. He threw his into the hedge and proceeded to haul, rolled up the flag, stuffed it into his belt, retrieved the gun, joined the other three and all mooched off. Maybe winners and losers all felt a bit like that, especially losers.

The flight the next morning was for the usual two and a half hours. A persistent hangover, from unaccustomed alcoholic beverages, made it feel longer. We flew mostly over cloud with occasional glimpses of the sea, eventually making landfall at the eastern end of Marseilles. We flew low along the waterfront, then headed inland to the airport. On landing, it happened. The whole machine took on a mighty list to port. I felt sure a tyre had burst. I deserved it after my rotten landing. Stan leapt out to investigate and I saw him heaving up under the wing-tip until the oleo in the undercarriage came unstuck and we regained our horizontal position. All was well. On stepping out from the aircraft, I was immediately attacked by the bitterly cold Mediterranean wind which blows at that time of year. Dressed, as we were, in tropical kit, we all suffered. We also suffered a dreadful meal in the airport restaurant. I'm quite sure it was horse, and not a very young one at that. As soon as possible we took off again, next stop Paris.

En route we all took turns at piloting, navigating and generally looking out as, one by one, we changed into our blue uniforms of more substantial and warmth-giving material. I only saw glimpses of the Rhone Valley, as we flew along, and made a mental note to return sometime to see some more of it. By the time Paris came into view, all three of us were very much on the lookout. Firstly, at the easily recognisable landmarks, Eiffel Tower, Arc de Triomphe and Notre Dame, and up on, Montmartre, Sacre Coeur, then a search for our destination, a tiny field on the outskirts, but mostly for all the other aeroplanes doing exactly what we were doing. French fighter aircraft in ragged formations prowled around below circuit height, odd foreign-looking planes scampered to and fro, a few Dakotas plodded on, and we tried dodging them all. We had landed by late afternoon and were whisked off to a hotel close to the Opera House.

Somehow, I managed to make refuelling and maintenance on the Expeditor last for three days, while I marched my crew from one sight-seeing 'must' to another, including the Follies Bergere, as part of their education. I, at least, had been to Paris a few times before the war and felt it my duty to show them as many good things as possible. We dragged ourselves away at last and were airborne after an early lunch at Le Buc, our Paris airfield.

We flew to Munich as mentioned previously, not in quite the most direct line, as I wanted to see the state of the German towns on the way. My operational flying had taken me over many, many German cities and towns, all at dead of night. The view I had of them then was looking through smoke, fire and bomb blast. From a distance, on that afternoon, Stuttgart, and all the other towns for that matter, looked fairly normal. The four and five-storied blocks of buildings stood there reflecting the low sun and looking a colourful yellow, white and brown. The staggering truth only became apparent when we were much closer. Every, and absolutely every, building was a derelict burnt-out shell - empty, deserted, crumbling and dead. A couple of years before I had watched these very places receive the treatment from the bomber force, but never realised how complete the destruction was. A bombing raid was a pretty lively occasion; now everything in sight was absolutely dead.

Munich was in the same state. The streets looked to be clear, where all rubble had been swept to the sides forming banks of bricks and masonry to around ten feet in height. We landed there, and by some miracle, it was one of the best landings I'd ever made. I didn't feel the wheels touch the ground. I was even congratulated by my crew.

This Munich aerodrome was next door to the Dornier factory, where I found, in the bombed-out hangars, some examples of the Dornier 335's. They were reckoned to be one of the fastest piston-engined aircraft ever produced by the German aircraft industry. They were all badly battered, although the peculiar arrangement of having an engine and propeller at the front and rear was still discernible. They were brought out too late ever to be a menace to the RAF. On the tarmac areas, now stood Flying Fortresses, Dakotas and Expeditors. Americans of all ranks scurried about in Jeeps, all in a desperate hurry to go somewhere or do something or other. After my leisurely forty flying hour flight of sheer bliss, I handed over Expeditor KJ 554 to the Americans. I had not really come to terms with the fact that my perfect landing was to be my very last landing executed by me in a service aeroplane.

The Americans made us most welcome during our short stay at OberLAAffenhofen, taking us to places of interest in Munich and district, and to some very drunken parties, before flying us to England in a Dakota.

The coach trip from Bovingdon aerodrome to central London, although short, gave me time to realise that every move from now on would be a move further and further away from aerodromes, aeroplanes and flying. I started to feel displeased with life. Stan's parents were very pleased when we managed to turn up at his place in Croydon just in time to celebrate his birthday.

The next day I trekked off to darkest Wiltshire, which was to be home for the next few years. After a week of waiting, I was summoned to the Demob centre in Stafford, fixed up with some ill-fitting clothing, given a railway pass, and from then on, I was out. For days ahead life became an unsure and unaccustomed existence.

With the end of the war and then demob there was more to do than just sit around looking glamorous in uniform or unglamorous in my demob suit. I had joined up for the duration of the war and felt my duty, in the future, lay in other directions.

CHAPTER THIRTEEN
My first crash

So much for big aeroplanes, but the biggest fright I've had so far was in a very small plane. This was in a Taylor Monoplane, a very small, fairly low-powered aeroplane, which I was asked to test-fly after finishing the SE5a. The test over a couple of days was going well, I'd managed many circuits and landings, climbs and stalls, and found it to be a lovely little plane. It had a tight-fitting cockpit which gave a great sense of togetherness where you only had to think it into a manoeuvre and off it went, like a little Spitfire.

After a few enjoyable days of testing, I was asked if I would deliver it to a somewhat small and remote strip a few miles from where I had been flying it. I could see the weather was not really good enough, breezy, gusty, a few showers and generally uncomfortable for flying in small open-cockpit machines. The owner was to follow me by car and pick me up.

After buzzing around the area where I was sure the strip should be, I spotted a windsock, a rigid yellow cone, straight out and at right angles to the strip where I had to land. I should have returned to the place from whence I came, but being over-confident (and stupid) I prowled around the circuit hoping the wind might drop a little. I can't go back of course, I'm a test pilot.

Gently, gently, we approached the strip. A little bit fast, kick off a bit of rudder to line it up, hold off and then – BANG! Unable to keep it straight the poor little plane had sheared off the slippery grass strip into the next field and overturned. I could feel the straps trying to pull me down onto the seat, but in no time I was upside-down and completely trapped in the tiny cockpit, shouting at myself for being such a BF, knowing full well it was my own silly fault.

All was very quiet, I could hear the petrol trickling from the tank, but try as I might I could neither move nor see anything except the damp ground pushing against my face. There was no escape. How long, I wondered, would my help-mate be driving to pick me up. As he had never been to the strip before he might have got lost. Lying there I could only think that when the fumes of the petrol reached the hot engine I would burn. I remembered a passage in Dickens' *Tale of Two Cities* when an aristocrat, who is lying beneath the hoisted blade of the guillotine, composes himself to accept the future with no sign of fear. In the film *Waldo Pepper* some poor chap is shouting his head off when he was caught underneath his burning plane, until his friend took out his gun and shot him. It kept him quiet! I seem to recall that in the First World War some pilots carried revolvers with them in case they were shot down in flames. I had no gun, so I just had to put up with it.

Thank God no fire erupted, and I had to put up with it for 45 minutes until I heard voices. I shouted, "I'm OK, no bones broken." Two or three policemen, plus the owner of the plane, lifted the port wing just enough for me to scramble out. I stood up, declaring that all was well, then started to feel giddy from being upside-down for so long and promptly fell down. All was well though, and I drove home after collecting my car from the aerodrome.

The unfortunate Taylor Monoplane

The local papers had a great time thinking up headlines like 'Ace breaks nose in crash' or 'Aircraft wheel goes down rabbit hole and overturns'. I have always been lucky and, being a bit thick, no frightening experiences have ever given me nightmares, even in wartime.

CHAPTER FOURTEEN
Post-war flying

I knew perfectly well that I was going to miss aeroplanes. I did not yet realise how much. There was a great feeling throughout society that now was the time for rebuilding. There were shortages in every direction. A number of crack-pot political schemes were proving disastrous, and the real essentials were only slowly getting under way. As an overgrown office boy with still no qualifications, except the ability to kill, I had little to offer. I felt the rebuilding of the British way of life was the most essential problem to be tackled. The year of 1947 turned out to be a turning point in my life. Everyone everywhere suffered one of the worst winters in living memory. My father, who had been threatening to do so for thirty years, died.

The late spring morning was beautiful, and spring in Wiltshire can be exceedingly beautiful. So there I was staying for a few days with Mum in quite a large farm in the country. Being a school teacher, she had dashed off to school in Lambourn, where she taught and had a class waiting for her to dish out the education. I crawled out of bed, crammed down a very basic breakfast and went out to my Austin 7 with the thought that I'd drive into Marlborough for lunch.

Then, as far as I was concerned - nothing, nothing and more nothing! For four days I had passed out - extremely out. People from the farm saw me staggering about, quite unable to speak and being horribly sick all over the place.

They considered I was drunk and were relieved when I went indoors again. "Let him sober up," they said.

I went to bed.

I was still there and still unconscious when Mum came home late in the afternoon and it didn't take long before she had telephoned the doctor in Ramsbury, the local village.

The doctor was a brilliant doctor AND, surprisingly, also a brilliant vet, and being a vet, he was used to diagnosing medical troubles without asking any questions. He diagnosed my trouble without even a grunt or a snort from me, summoned the ambulance and whisked me into Marlborough Hospital.

I do remember 'coming to' for a second or two with a great pain in my hip. I later found out why; a very hot, hot-water bottle had blistered my hip. Fortunately, I passed out again and felt nothing more for a few days. I knew very little of what was going on, except screens being placed around my bed and some TLC being given by a pretty nurse, who initially thought I was a child all curled up in my bed clothes, but was somewhat frightened when I turned to her and displayed my large RAF moustache.

I must have recovered rather slowly, and one day, when I realised I badly needed a pee, I crawled out of bed still in a dozy state and was found by the same pretty nurse in the Ladies lav. I was ushered out.

The doctors told Mum that I'd suffered from a sub-arachnoid haemorrhage, which means I'd had a busted blood vessel somewhere close to my brain. There was a lot of talk about possible 'brain damage'. Didn't they know that 'brain damage' is essential if you volunteer to become a pilot? Mum visited every day and the vicar occasionally visited as well; I'm sure he was convinced I was going to snuff it. Having seen and spoken to the pretty nurse a few times, I'd made up my mind I was NOT going to snuff it.

The hospital routine plodded on. There were ward maids, who I thought were brought from some sort of asylum to help with the menial tasks, vary caring people, but who spoke a strange sort of English. At the end of dinner, one would stand at the end of the ward and shout, "Anybody want any more pudden?" or, "Done yer tea?" At evening they would remove all vases of flowers to stop them breathing our air at night.

I discovered my nurse was called 'Liz', and after a long time I married the girl. It took ages to convince her that this idiot she had returned to life was the right one. We've now been married for sixty-three years, maybe we did the right thing, though I'm still treated like a child.

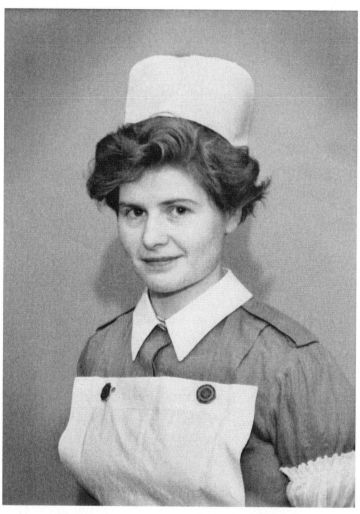

The pretty nurse, now Doug's wife, Liz

I was subsequently told by the RAF doctors that the illness was probably caused by test flying, that I would never fly again and had to leave the RAF Volunteer Reserve. I conveniently forgot their diagnosis and, as you have gathered, I flew again.

My mother, as I have said, had returned to her profession as a schoolteacher at the beginning of the war. Her father had been a teacher in his younger days. Many of my aunts and uncles were in the same profession. Cousins by the cart-load were following the trend, so I suppose it was not unnatural that I should choose to become yet another bearer of the education torch. The three 'R's have always been punched into children, and rightly so. The belief by educationalists and parents, that excellence in that direction was essential for 'a good job', worried me a little. I felt that to be consciously aware of the aesthetic values in life could well be neglected for the race to material gain. Having met plenty of characters who had been educated in such a one-sided way, I realised what they had been missing, even if they did not. I had always had an interest in art at school, and drama outside school, I had run art societies within the RAF and taken part in things theatrical whilst in the service. Consequently, I took a college course, with art and drama as my main subjects. Whether I learned much was doubtful, but at least I managed to gain a qualification, which kept me in an underpaid job for the rest of my working life. Obviously, the quest to earn a crust cut down on any flying activities.

The same year that I got married, I started gliding. An army club who flew from Old Sarum, near Salisbury, very decently allowed some interested civilians to join them to fly their T 21 elementary glider. I was lucky enough to be included. The actual flying presented no difficulty, and in no time I had soloed. I have, since then, been taking part in gliding, on and off, for years, but still have the thought, at the back of my mind, that I need an engine in front.

I would still recommend gliding as a splendid way to get to know about the mysteries of aviation. Spending all day on the gliding site, listening to the experts and watching the inexpert, is the right kind of education for would-be aviators. If you stand all day in the weather, and not sit ignoring it from the inside of the clubhouse, you'll soon get to know what it is all about and what it can do for you when you climb up into it. Airfields are great places for seeing the weather coming.

After some considerable time, that is enough time to earn enough to pay for flying hours, I joined several local flying clubs and continued my addiction. The Auster, a type of aircraft I had tested in India, was often the backbone of the clubs. I had never been terribly smitten with their performance, especially the low-engine-powered ones. Even the more powerful marks seemed to be unpredictable in my hands. Some days all was well and they did as I requested, yet at other times they appeared to have minds of their own, and try as I might, nothing would go right. The Austers with the Cirrus Minor engines were very underpowered if any more than one person was carried, the square-engined version, difficult to see out of, the J1N more difficult to land than the Mark 6, and the Aerocar heavy. Having run the poor things down, I have to admit to a growing liking for them after the first four hundred hours in them.

Most of that time was spent in glider-towing with a naval gliding club. On joining that club, I was allowed into the Auster tug syndicate. That meant working hard, towing good and bad glider pilots and their various mounts to a couple of thousand feet up, catching a thermal if possible, and letting them release into rising air. Weekend after weekend the towing continued, never more than a few miles from base. I was getting the urge to explore a little further afield. I wondered if any of the other tug pilots ever flew further than our immediate vicinity. Some were keen to do so, especially Des, who was a little more adventurous than the rest.

Soon we started short cross-country flights to places of interest. Our excursions got longer, until eventually we managed to fly in short stages from the south of England to the Scottish border, calling at large and small aerodromes, and all without radio. The country was, and still is, dotted with airfields which light aircraft can visit. Most are friendly, but there will always be some little chaps who come dashing out to tell you that you have infringed some petty rule. They must be allowed to enjoy their power without ruining your day.

The business of drawing a line on a map and then flying along it until the destination turns up, amazes the novice. The ability to fly an accurate compass course while carefully map-reading is the essence of this kind of navigation. In light aircraft, radio aids should be classed as aids only and not form the only method of navigation. It is possible - it has happened to me - that the electrics can all pack up, leaving one in an 'I don't know where I am' situation. Finding one's way does not always work out quite as it should and I would be telling a big fib if I said I had never been lost.

In the early 1970's the Royal Navy gave up using Tiger Moths. I believe they had really given them up years before, but kept a few on for navigational exercises. These few left their West Country base and were distributed to various clubs, museums and other places. We, the gliding club at Lee-on-Solent, were lucky enough to have one join us. It was a delight to fly a Tiger again. Soon Des and I became the main maintenance workers for this machine, and for seven years put in a vast number of hours keeping it in an airworthy condition. We also flew it. It was sacrilege to use this aeroplane for towing gliders, but that was the way of things, so tow it did. Fortunately, we did manage to take it away on many occasions, touring the country, visiting fly-ins, attending air shows and generally doing what should be done in Tiger Moths. On one such occasion we did meet a toffee-nosed chap who slithered out from his immaculately preserved Naval aeroplane to complain to us that our machine was dirty and a disgrace. He was right, it was dirty, from hard work. I wondered how often he had ever cleaned his. When these deities strike, it is best to turn the other cheek so that they can't see the giggles.

Although the Tiger is not the greatest aerobatic machine, we had great fun throwing it about. It would loop, spin and stall turn beautifully, but roll badly. We were allowed to take part in a couple of air races. First, the 'Round the Island' race, the island being the Isle of Wight. Our handicap put us in the front for take-off. In fact, I think we had completed a circuit of the island before the fast machines had taken off. We ended well down the field at the finish, but it was a great thrill, charging round the island's coast, shaving the Needles' light, and steep-turning around the forts in the Solent.

Our next race was the King's Cup. Again, the dubious pleasure of starting first. Of course, we finished last, having flown more of the race than anyone else.

My affection for Tigers started way back in the forties with 'O.B.' in Rhodesia, It continued with the squadron hack, continued again with the Group Captain's Tiger in India, and then again at Lee. What a shame some misguided person at Lee, who obviously had little soul, managed to get rid of this light of my life.

I oft recall, boring the pants off those who have heard the story before, the tale of the epic flight in the squadron Tiger during the winter of 1944.

In February 1944, I was on 141 Squadron at West Raynham, near Fakenham in Norfolk, flying operations on Mosquitos. I can't remember why it was, but I had urgent business in Southampton and could not afford to be away from West Raynham for too long. I managed to persuade my Flight Commander that a trip to Southampton was a must, and would he allow me to fly down for the day in, of all things, the squadron's Tiger Moth? Steve, ever faithful, elected to come along, even though the business was for my benefit. He considered he had best navigate so as to make sure I returned in one piece.

Winter in England is cold. Winter in East Anglia is colder, and this particular day was well above average cold. We dressed in battledress, with long johns beneath and Irvin jackets and flying boots above, refueled the Tiger, checked the oil, stuffed maps into the tops of the flying boots, donned gloves, swung the prop and set off. At eighty miles per hour the ground passed very slowly below us. We had started off before the Met office was fully manned, although they did predict poor weather in the offing.

Maybe here I should give a little explanation of some of the drawbacks we had to cope with in our aeroplane. First and foremost there was no communication between the two cockpits. Shouting as loud as you like would not be heard, so we had instigated a method of navigation. Steve would read the map while I concentrated on flying the machine on a pre-arranged series of courses we had drawn up at base. If he noticed any deviation Steve would tap the joystick either left or right to get us back on track.

All appeared to be jogging along quite nicely, though I was

soon frozen stiff and I'm sure Steve was as well. Near Huntingdon I noticed not only the cloud lowering, but the ground getting white. Flying through a misty atmosphere I didn't realise it was real snow, but it was. If things stayed as they were I was sure it would be quite all right, as long as I could see ahead and pick out the odd landmark, so we pressed on.

So far the east wind had been pushing us along in the direction we wanted to go, but as we were flying faster than the wind, we were catching up with the weather front which bore the snow clouds. On we flew into lowering clouds. Where we had been flying at 1500 feet above the ground, we had had to descend so as to be able to see forward any distance.

Somewhere near Luton I reckoned things were getting a bit out of hand, if not downright dangerous. I was down to around 200 feet when I decided enough was enough when the road I had been following went up a hill and disappeared into the cloud. It was time to get down on the ground.

I had thought about forced landings before and had decided on one or two 'musts'. Firstly, a stretch of ground, long and flat enough without any obstacles on approach or overshoot. Secondly, it had to be near civilisation; there was little point being on the ground miles away from any road, house or sign of life. By now, at just over treetop height, with the ground covered by a blanket of snow and with my world restricted to a small circle of visibility, immediate action was necessary, and we were fortunate to find, without too much looking, a large country house, not quite a mansion, but near enough, with a field long enough for the Tiger to land. Of the surface we knew nothing, it might have been grass, mud, ploughed or anything else, whatever it was we had little choice but to land and take a chance. I did a circuit and bounced the wheels onto the ground. All seemed well. I imagined that whatever it was, it would have been frozen pretty hard. The actual landing was better than my usual ones, probably because the snow acted as a cushion.

Stopping well before the end of the field, I swung the Tiger round and taxied back, ready for the next take-off. Getting out was a struggle, our bodies were frozen stiff and it was only after jumping about and flapping our arms that circulation returned and we felt well enough to congratulate ourselves for getting down in one piece.

Bordering our field was a narrow country road, which separated us from the large house which I had targeted, so we made our way towards the boundary hedge and were mightily surprised when a loud voice broke the silence with the words "Hello, hello." Before us was a large snow-covered policeman, pushing a large snow-covered bicycle.

Again, "Hello, hello, where have you come from and what are you doing here?" I wanted to say, "We're from Mars and what's it to do with you?" But instead we tried to explain that we were not Germans or spies or, as our policeman thought, trainees. With a scribbled note in his snow-sodden book and a disgruntled murmur, he pushed his way along his snowy beat while we carried on towards the house.

The ageing couple welcomed us in, and over cups of tea we explained our reasons for dropping in, although stupidly, we failed to ask where we were. Of course, as RAF officers we were not lost, but the actual address of the house remains a mystery, although we think it was somewhere near Offley, in Hertfordshire.

Within half an hour the snow stopped falling, as I imagine the weather front had moved on westward, so it was time to leave our fire, say our thanks and get back into the cold.

Steve only had to swing the propeller a few times to get the engine started. I let it warm up a bit to get the oil circulating and we were off again up into the freezing air. Back on course all seemed well, until once again the cloud lowered and we were flying between layers. I felt sure that if I could get above the top layer I would be in sunshine, so I climbed up through the cloud, not easy with the limited instrumentation on the Tiger Moth. I eventually emerged at 4,000 feet into the light.

I knew at some time I would have to land to refuel and, after watching the gauge decrease, I descended back through the cloud, hoping I would break cloud before we hit the ground.

We broke cloud at 1,000 feet above a white world, and it was not long before I saw an aerodrome with a few American aircraft parked on the apron. This was Aldermaston, long before it became atomic. The American GI who met us there exploded with mirth, shouting, "Gee guys, a box-kite!" I'll admit it did look a bit odd amongst the Lightning fighters. I thought at the time it was a bit of an unnecessary remark, but said nothing except, "Thanks for the petrol."

Off we went again and the next stop would be Eastleigh aerodrome, near Southampton, although in 1944 it was HMS *Raven*, a Naval establishment. Good old south coast, the weather was clear with glimpses of the sun, so navigation was easy. Leaving St Catherine's Hill at Winchester on our left, we flew down the railway until we could see Southampton Water, and there we were. I did a quick circuit, landed, and taxied in, to be met by an overweight Chief Petty Officer, who with all the pomposity he could muster, shouted, "You can't land here."

Trying to explain that I had just done so, did not convince this landlubber sailor that I could break his law quite so easily. Apparently, I should have first landed at Worthy Down, another land-based ship called HMS *Kestrel*, to find out if the balloon barrage was in operation. I had found it quite easy to miss them, unlike the German Me109s who never missed shooting them down just before the bombs fell on Southampton.

Poor old Southampton High Street, a place I knew having worked as an office boy in a solicitor's office just off the main thoroughfare, had been badly bombed. Fortunately, Lyon's Tea Shop was still there and open, so we had cups of tea and a rather solid bun before the small matter of business for which we had come this far was completed and we were ready for a return trip by taxi to the aerodrome.

Double British Summer Time was in operation, which meant that although it was past tea time there would still be a couple of hours of daylight left in the evening. It was still jolly cold, although the early afternoon was a bit brighter. The south-west wind hurried our progress. A quick stop at Bovingdon for fuel and off again.

I was becoming more and more certain that it would be dark before we got to West Raynham. I reckoned to fly on into the night, using dead-reckoning navigation then putting down as near as possible to base. I calculated that with a full tank of petrol, careful navigation and a bit of luck, we could get back to Norfolk before it got too dark. Once again navigation was Steve's job, with a tap on the joystick left or right to keep me on track. Thank God the weather had cleared, snow still covered the ground, but visibility was good and the only cloud was fairly high, so at least half the journey passed without incident, although it was getting dark.

No more taps on the stick meant either I was on track or Steve could not see any more landmarks. The red and green navigation lights just showed their reflections on the Tiger's wing tips, but all else was blackness, save for the occasional ring of circuit lights of some unknown (to me) aerodrome.

On and on we went; by now I could no longer see the petrol gauge, which is a small float on the top wing, but I had been airborne long enough for the Tiger's endurance to be running out. The calculated time for the trip had expired, I had no accurate idea as to our position, but knew we must be somewhere near our destination, and also that if I kept on flying I would end up over the North Sea. I decided to land at the very next lighted aerodrome and within minutes of my decision a ring of lights appeared dead ahead, a very welcome sight, with the outer ring of the Drem System lights (a system of airfield lighting developed at and named after the RAF station in Scotland where I had done an emergency landing) and the actual straight flight path. I could see no other traffic's navigation lights, so with one quick circuit of the station I landed. All went well until the tail went down and we came to an abrupt halt. It felt like landing on an aircraft carrier when the arrester wire catches the tail hook of the aircraft.

Try as I might, with a great deal of throttle I could not move, so I stopped the engine and got out to find what was causing the problem. Something like Somerfield Tracking, the squares of wire mesh used to reinforce grass runways, had been laid out on the runway, and the tailskid of the Tiger had been caught up by it. We had to drag the Tiger backwards, lift the tail up and then push it off the runway onto the grass surrounding. Once we had done this and restarted the engine, I made my way, with Steve walking in front to look out for pot-holes or obstructions, to the parking area by the control tower.

Although we had held up a stack of Wellington bombers from landing and kept them going round in circles for some time, we were forgiven by the controller at Coltishall, which is where we had arrived, a bit off course and a little too close to the North Sea. He knew us from our usual operational visits with our Mosquito.

Next morning, after rising early, we had enough fuel left to fly the twenty-odd miles west to West Raynham by ten o'clock the next morning.

Looking back, I should have known better than to have gone to Southampton in the first place. Why Steve continued flying with such an idiot is beyond me.

The Lee-on-Solent Tiger put us into a somewhat similar situation, when in March 1973 Des and I delivered a glider to Nymphsfield, then continued on to try to find a small airstrip in the Wye Valley. Snow again had us landing in a field, this time the piece of ground recently reclaimed from open-cast mining and nicely flat. After a wait for the weather we got off again and eventually found the strip, where the owner was standing in the snow, shining his green Aldis lamp. The wind-sock had disappeared in the gale the day before, giving us no clue as to where his landing-ground might be. It was a very small strip; I'm glad he was there. I cannot ever remember being so cold as I was during that flight. I took so long to warm up, I'm sure I must have been in the first, if not the last, stages of hypothermia.

That same Tiger caught us out on another occasion when it decided to oil up both the plugs on one cylinder, giving a substantial loss of power and making the most awful complaining noises. Down we came, this time onto a steep hillside. The steep slope upwards quickly brought us to a halt. The next day we corrected things and took off from the top of the hill. It was like being shot off from a catapult. This all happened at the small village of Warnford, just to the north of Portsmouth, and named, I believe, after a famous flyer of the First World War.

Everyone who has flown Tiger Moths has a pet Tiger story or two. Mine could fill a book, some good, some bad and some best forgotten.

The next Tiger which came into my life belonged to the Bustard Flying Club. This club took its name from the large birds which at one time inhabited Salisbury Plain. The station RAF Boscombe Down has these birds incorporated into its badge, and as the club originated from Boscombe Down, it follows that the name of the club should embody these birds.

The Bustard Flying Club was formed by some bright, high-ranking officers of RAF Boscombe Down, who enjoyed light aircraft flying as a pastime and as a diversion from test flying in the Empire Test Pilots' School. They procured a couple of Tiger Moths, and while Old Sarum aerodrome was still under the jurisdiction of the services, started the club there.

Flying from the grassy undulating field of Old Sarum had a real club feel about it. They worried no-one and probably found it a wonderful break from the sophisticated machines at Boscombe Down. Bill Goldfinch was invited to join, as the first civilian, in the very early days of the club. It was to Old Sarum that he took his immaculately-built Luton Minor, after he had constructed most of it in his lounge. I remember it took quite a long time to build, so that after a while it was classed as a piece of the home furniture.

I was the third person to fly it. The act of getting into it was like following a knitting pattern - an in, over, through, off, put two together formula would eventually get you past most of the wire and into the cockpit. It flew well, though the Jap engine's horse power was made up from horses which should have been taken to the knacker's yard years before. I loved sitting in the open cockpit with the wing above keeping the rain off.

After many hours flying, Bill decided to install a Volkswagen engine in the hope of gaining a little more performance and less demand on the servicing. After fitting the new power plant, the Luton Minor remained a treat to fly, but the performance was little different - forty-five miles per hour was no speed for getting anywhere, and the rate of climb was not too good. There was no doubt it kept you on your toes the whole time, where the slightest loss of concentration meant a loss of height. Taking off towards the west at Old Sarum necessitated bearing off to the right to avoid hitting the Old Sarum castle, and if airborne in a stiff breeze, flying upwind, as a leg downwind might mean running short of petrol before regaining the aerodrome. Using thermals, I did, on one occasion, manage to climb to three thousand five hundred feet. I felt pretty clever. Since those days Bill changed mounts to a two-seat Jodel. He prowled around the country, enjoying his flying as much as I did, until his death in 2007.

Des and I were lucky enough to become members of the very select Bustard Flying Club some years ago. The all-black Tiger Moth was not being used a great deal, so I think the club decided to allow some old ex-RAF types to join. We used it on as many occasions as possible and notched up some excellent trips in G-ALND.

Unfortunately, that was at a time in aviation history when the Tiger Moth was condemned as old, draughty, slow, uncomfortable, expensive to run and difficult to maintain, and was generally disliked by those who craved comfort and the ability to go from A to B. It was not surprising that the thought within the club was to get rid of the old black beast and get a more modern aircraft. The Tiger was sold, plus enough spares to build another, and a Jodel 1050 took its place.

Des and I were extremely sorry to see the Tiger go. It looked so right when it was either sitting in the old First World War hangar at Old Sarum, or flying from that lovely grass which suited the Tiger so well.

I took an immediate dislike to the Jodel, considering it to be too close to a 'spam can' for my liking. I must quickly say that that dislike soon disappeared when I found out how useful the Jodel could be. It will never be the fun aeroplane that the Tiger was, but for journeys of over a few miles, it has the edge. With three people aboard and still room for some baggage, it will cruise economically at just over one hundred miles per hour and use around five gallons of petrol per hour. I can see why the Jodels, in all their various marks and numbers, are so popular. They must be one of the best kinds of little aeroplanes for cruising about in.

What a pity the British aircraft industry couldn't build anything as good.

America has, up to now, led the way in large and small non-military aeroplanes using metal construction, and as aerial motor cars they have been most successful. We for some reason always tried to copy them. The Jodel didn't. Simple wooden construction has a lot going for it, as long as it is kept in a hangar and out of the most severe weather.

The Bustard's Jodel lived in a hangar until 'Optica' took over Old Sarum. They kindly allowed us to stay in their hangars until they needed them for workshops in which to build their revolutionary observation aeroplane.

We moved first into the open for a few months, until the Dorset Gliding Club let us use one end of their canvas hangar. We were dry again. Moving the Bustard Flying Club into Boscombe Down, became inevitable. It is a Boscombe Down club run mainly by Boscombe Down people with a strong membership of crown servants and serving RAF people. I am appreciative of the fact that I am allowed to be a member. The decision to move was made by the high-ups, so move we did.

A long-standing rule of the club dictates that if any private owner keeps an aeroplane beneath the shadow of the club, it may be flown by club members who may wish to do so. Under that rule I took my S.E.5a to Boscombe Down, after first getting the blessing and permission of the top man. I hoped the RAF would not think it a retrogressive step to have an S.E.5a on the same station as their Hawks and Tornadoes. Fortunately, club aeroplanes only fly after the bigger and faster planes are put away. We then share the aerodrome with aeromodellers and a few stray pheasants.

CHAPTER FIFTEEN
The Great War Display Team

It was not long after my first flight in my S.E.5a that Des Biggs and Ken Garrett also finished their S.E.5as and we did some formation flying together. Somehow, the BBC found out about us, and when we were to perform at Biggin Hill, they interviewed us for their early morning TV programme, not just to see the aeroplanes, but also the odd characters who flew them. Somehow this seemed to trigger off invitations to perform some kind of aerial dancing around the skies, which we hoped was to the enjoyment and wonder of the air show crowds.

Doug and Des fly their S.E.5a biplanes

Even more excitement was caused by the introduction of a Fokker Triplane, initially for many years a lovely red one flown by Robin Bowes from Ermington in Devon. Unfortunately, Robin died in an unexplained accident whilst flying his lovely aircraft with us at a display at Stourhead. We then were joined by a black one from the Army Air Corps Museum, flown by Nick O'Brien, a real expert pilot from Middle Wallop AAC base. We were also fortunate enough to find an RAF Wing Commander called Chris Mann, who, when not flying RAF aeroplanes, joined us in some of our shows in his S.E.5a. These two were not only good and experienced pilots, but they had a great knowledge of display flying, which Des and I did not have.

We needed a triplane, an English one, and by now Ernie Holbyn had completed rebuilding his Sopwith Triplane, which evened up the display team's complement.

The Great War Display Team at Biggin Hill

The team was now known as The Great War Display Team, and it grew to a considerable size, operating at airshows, not only in the South of England, but on occasions as far afield as Yorkshire, France and even Northern Ireland. Airshow organisers soon found it an advantage having an aircraft team who put on a performance rather than simply having a nice aircraft whizzing past. We tried to put on a show and by increasing our flock we had quite a lot to offer.

Our Team increased in number until we had, at our peak, two Triplanes, one English and one German, a Nieuport, two Junkers, several S.E.5as and a Sopwith Pup. We occasionally linked up with some actors from the Chelsea Hospital show and some Re-enactors, all in authentic uniforms, with bell-tents, field kitchens, workshops and all manner of First World War equipment. They marched, and even had church parades with a real vicar, a flag-lowering ceremony at the end of the day, and then they went off to sleep in their tents. We snobs nipped off to the local hotels of course.

After nearly 900 flying hours in my S.E.5a and getting so old, some people asked if I really did fly in the Great War. I decided to let the younger ones carry on flying at air shows without me. They probably said, "Thank God for that."

Liz helping push the S.E.5a into taxi position

Two very different trips spring to mind about the time when I was flying with the Team, which only really concerned a couple of aircraft. The first involved the aircraft being static background scenery, the second a short fly-past.

I was extremely pleased when Air Commodore Dye, whom I met at the Royal International Air Tattoo at Fairford, asked if I could bring my replica S.E.5a to St. Omer in northern France, to be part of the backdrop at the unveiling by a vast collection of bigwigs from the RAF and French Air Force, of the memorial to the aircrew of the RFC who were lost in the Great War.

The memorial is actually on the site of the WWI flying field, which is still used as an aerodrome. Somehow the local press, local radio and local television got word of this adventure, and so pictures and comments were in the press, interviews on the TV, and South Today sent a cameraman/reporter to Popham aerodrome to film the operation from readiness to take-off. John Day, who is about half my age, made the other half of the memorial backdrop. He and I flew in formation to St. Omer, he in his beautiful Nieuport 17 and me in my S.E.5a, with a Junkers CL1 flown by Bob Gauld-Galliers, which was needed to carry all the equipment.

My wife Liz was there at Popham to get me off, but after the final goodbye wave she returned to the car to drive home and realized that I had flown off with the car keys. The TV chap was delighted to be able to film Liz saying a few choice words.

Flying little light aeroplanes can be something like a bicycle ride, whichever way you go you will have a mighty headwind. Crossing the channel at an average of around 55mph, the white horses looked most uninviting. St. Omer was delightful, good grass for the landing, good hangarage and, above all, super people.

I was somewhat led astray by these young fellers whose bedtime was way past my own, so that on returning to the hotel at an unearthly hour on the Thursday night we found entry was bolted and barred. I will not mention how they got in, but suffice to say that I came in through the back door.

Friday was rehearsal day. The RAF central band was magnificent, the RAF regiment marchers were as good as any Guards regiment, and the French contingent took part. We flew for the cameras, and in the afternoon an RAF helicopter had us up flying formation around the French countryside. I was most impressed with the whole organisation where the bods of the various media used hours of whatever they put their pictures on.

Next day, with the two aeroplanes in position beside the rather beautiful memorial, the long drawn-out unveiling ceremony took place. The French do go on! Eventually, the bands played and we all had a bit of a get-together with Champers and grub.

Another surprise was to come across the grandson of Lord Trenchard, the father of the RAF in the Great War. I had met the great Lord himself in 1944 when he visited my Squadron to give us all a friendly chat.

One more point about St Omer, in the last war the Luftwaffe had taken over the aerodrome and sent their Me109s to England. One day they found my squadron, which was equipped with Boulton-Paul Defiant aircaft. Many of the poor things were shot down or badly damaged and the Squadron was withdrawn from the Battle of Britain. Fortunately, this was before I joined the squadron.

Sunday morning, we were out with the aeroplanes and off into a mighty headwind. Channel crossing even longer. Apprehension when the controller at Popham radioed that Liz was there waiting, actually with no rolling pin.

To sum up, I was so glad to have been able to attend such a wonderful occasion, so glad to have met such wonderful people and so glad to have been looked after by John and Bob, who I think classed me as Grandad. If I'm not careful I'll be feeling my age!

The second memorable trip was to the Somme memorial at Thiepval, along with Ernie Hoblyn in his Sopwith Triplane. We flew over to Abbeville, and the next day we flew on to the vast memorial in very bumpy and most uncomfortable weather. We flew by at the proper time and then flew home again, having done what was required of us. It was only later I saw, on TV, the piper leading in the crowds of VIPs, and then the Prince of Wales clapping his hands with glee as we staggered by.

POSTSCRIPT

When one's ninetieth birthday passes and folks say, "The old fool's still about," it's time for wondering why heaven or hell has not demanded attendance. Possibly because neither side has any desire to put up with someone who can only keep on about how wonderful flying has become. After all, heaven knows all about flying, and hell's boss can only recall a diving descent when he displeased the No1 God.

So I continue to try to remember the good bits, and am only too pleased to brag that I have flown ninety-odd aeroplanes and flown into, and out of, two hundred and fifty aerodromes in England, Africa, India, Europe – and even Scotland. I suppose I should say 'landed' at all these places, and landed might well be true, though some landings were more horrendous than others. As my first instructor said, "Hold the wheels six inches above the ground and let the 'plane stall on to it." This is only easy if one is sure where the ground is and whether the particular aircraft has decided to put up with your feeble ability. So far, after so many thousands of flying hours, I can only claim about three landings which I could describe as 'perfect'. Many ground crews have been extremely kind and never mentioned the poor arrivals, even though I have noticed some inspecting the undercarriage. Comments range from good to bad, depending how they feel at the time.

Pilots who rarely flew were asked by the ground crew if they might cut the grass around the aircraft's wheels, whereas, if you overused a plane you drew the comment, "Not again please, you'll wear out your piece of sky." My general feeling for these ground crew chaps, and often young ladies, is a great sense of devotion to the plane and its pilot.

In 1947, after my time in hospital when for some reason this blood-bursting brain business happened, I took no notice of the RAF doctors when they declared, "You'll never fly again." I flew again, and loved almost every minute of the thrill of it.

I'd love to keep on flying until I snuff it, but unfortunately it causes such difficulties pushing the plane out of the hangar, for both Liz and myself, who neither of us have anything like the energy we had a few years ago. I have difficulty reaching the propeller to start it, and one day I can see myself going round with it when it does start. Long distance flying is out now, as I get pretty tired trying to concentrate on all the business of flying, as well as navigating, dealing with the radio and all the present-day gadgetry which seems to be required for modern flying.

I wonder, is it time to hang up my helmet and goggles? Maybe just one more flight!

My Grandad's Cool

I asked my old Grandad what he did when a lad
He said, "Can't remember all those years ago."
Mum said, "He won the War," at least she thought he had
So I suppose she really ought to know.
She said when he was young he used to fly a plane
She said he was a Brylcreem boy, whatever that may be.
Grandad said, "I guess she's right, I must have been insane."
Then Grandad mumbled softly "Gawd, was it me?"

Did you fly a Spitfire, Grandad, like my Airfix kit
And did you meet old Biggles, or Churchill, or the King
And did you shoot down a Focke Wulf, or a Messerschmitt
And did you see Dame Vera Lynn when she used to sing?
Tell me about it Grandad, I really want to know.
One chap at school says his Gramp was at the D Day do,
Mum said she knew that you had had a go.
Were you one of those old fellers too?

I watched them march in Normandy on the box
With all their ribbons shining in the sun.
Were you one of those meandering old crocks
and where are all the medals which you must have won?
Grandad said when he gets time he'll write it in a book.
I wanted to ask him lots more, but Mum said, "Don't."
She could see he'd got that tired look.

I'd love to think he'll write it down
But I'm pretty sure he won't.

Liz and Doug with the S.E.5a in 2012

PICTURE INDEX